AIR CAMPAIGN

KOREA 1950–53

B-29s, Thunderjets and Skyraiders fight the
strategic bombing campaign

MICHAEL NAPIER | ILLUSTRATED BY MADS BANGSØ

OSPREY PUBLISHING
Bloomsbury Publishing Plc
Kemp House, Chawley Park, Cumnor Hill, Oxford OX2 9PH, UK
29 Earlsfort Terrace, Dublin 2, Ireland
1385 Broadway, 5th Floor, New York, NY 10018, USA
E-mail: info@ospreypublishing.com
www.ospreypublishing.com

OSPREY is a trademark of Osprey Publishing Ltd

First published in Great Britain in 2023

A catalogue record for this book is available from the British Library.

ISBN: PB 9781472855558; eBook 9781472855527;
ePDF 9781472855534; XML 9781472855541

23 24 25 26 27   10 9 8 7 6 5 4 3 2 1

Maps by www.bounford.com
Diagrams by Adam Tooby
3D BEVs by Paul Kime
Index by Janet Andrew
Typeset by PDQ Digital Media Solutions, Bungay, UK
Printed and bound in India by Replika Press Private Ltd.

For title page caption, please see page 81.

AIR CAMPAIGN

CONTENTS

INTRODUCTION

A Boeing B-29 Superfortress medium bomber of the 98th Bombardment Group flies above the clouds over North Korea. The B-29 gave FEAF the ability to reach long-range strategic targets. (US National Archive)

Just before dawn on Sunday, June 25, 1950, under cover of an artillery barrage, ten divisions of North Korean troops of the Korean People's Army (KPA), supported by tanks and aircraft, swarmed across the 38th Parallel near Kaesong and Chuncheon. Taken completely by surprise, the poorly equipped South Korean forces of the Republic of Korea Army (ROKA) fought back bravely, but its units were swiftly overwhelmed by the North Korean assault. Thus started a war which would cover the whole length of the Korean peninsula within the next few months, before reaching a stalemate almost exactly on the pre-war border. The war then played out its violent course over the next two years, before an armistice brought an end to open hostilities. Throughout the conflict, air power played a key role in shaping the battlefield and applying strategic pressure to North Korean and Chinese troops and politicians. This book describes the strategic employment of air power by United Nations Command (UNC) during the Korean War.

Background to the war

Although it took the world by surprise, the outbreak of the Korean War was an almost inevitable result of the geo-political influences in the region over the previous 50 years. The history of Korea reflects its geography, and over the centuries the country has periodically found itself caught in the midst of the struggles between its powerful neighbors. Korea lies on a peninsula which runs on a north–south axis extending southwards from northeastern China (Manchuria) and is bounded by the Yellow Sea to the west and the Sea of Japan to the east. With a length of around 550 miles and a width of about 250 miles, it is roughly the same size as California. The northern border with China runs along the Yalu (Amnok) River in the northwest and the Tumen River in the northeast, but the lower reaches of the Tumen River also mark a short boundary with eastern Russia. To the south, the Korea Strait, just 150 miles wide at its narrowest point, separates the country from Japan. Thus, Korea lies at the focal point of the three major powers in the region: China, Japan and Russia. Japan had first assimilated Korea as a Japanese protectorate in 1905 before annexing the country completely five years later. Over the following years, there was strong resistance against Japanese rule both within and outside the country. An independent government in exile, the pseudo-democratic Provisional Government of the Republic of Korea, was formed in Shanghai, under the leadership of Syngman Rhee and anti-Japanese guerilla groups operated in northern parts of Korea. The latter included the communist-inspired Northeast Anti-Japanese United Army, of which Kim Il-sung was a key member.

At the end of World War II, the Soviets and Americans agreed to use the 38th Parallel as the demarcation between their respective spheres of interest. Initially, Korea was governed by a US–Soviet joint commission, but each side manoeuvred to install their own client governments. In 1948, the Republic of Korea (ROK) was established in South Korea under Syngman Rhee, while North Korea became the communist-inspired Democratic People's

Kim Il-sung, the North Korean leader who believed that he could reunite Korea as a communist country by means of a swift and decisive invasion of the South. (Bettmann/Getty Images)

Republic of Korea (DPRK) under the leadership of Kim Il-sung. Neither of the Korean governments recognized the other as being legitimate and both claimed sovereignty over the other's territory. Border clashes were not infrequent, but Soviet forces left the country in 1948 and the following year US military forces were also withdrawn. A perception that, having left the country, the Americans would not return to intervene, led the North Koreans to believe that they could defeat the ROK in a swift pre-emptive strike and reunify Korea under the banner of the DPRK. This view was also shared by Josef Stalin, and in early 1950 Kim Il-sung was given approval by Stalin to carry out an invasion.

Taking place at the junction point of Chinese, Soviet and American interests, the North Korean invasion might easily have been a trigger for a World War III. However, all three powers realized that it was in their best interests to limit the conflict to the Korean peninsula and not to provoke one another. Both the USA and USSR were still suffering the cost of World War II and China had only just emerged from a brutal civil war; furthermore, the USSR had yet to procure nuclear weapons. For these reasons, Soviet participation in the Korean War was kept secret and the Chinese troops were allegedly 'volunteers' forming the Chinese People's Volunteer Army (CPVA) rather than regular troops. Similarly, the USA justified its intervention under the auspices of the United Nations (UN), an international body which, significantly, did not include the People's Republic of China at that time and which was being boycotted by the USSR. The coalition of UN forces which fought in and over Korea was placed under command of the UNC.

After its surprise invasion on June 25, the KPA advanced steadily southwards, until it was held on the Pusan (now Busan) perimeter in the southeast corner of Korea at the end of July. After building up its forces, the UNC commenced an offensive on September 15 with a simultaneous breakout from the Pusan perimeter and large-scale amphibious landings at Inchon (Incheon) near Seoul, which was well behind the KPA lines. Now it was the turn of the UNC to make rapid advances and UNC troops reached the Yalu River in mid-October.

Lt Gen George E. Stratemeyer commanded the USAF Far East Air Force (FEAF) at the outbreak of the Korean War. (US National Archive)

At this stage, the Chinese intervened and the CPVA started a series of offensives through the winter of 1950–51 which drove the UNC troops back south. Seoul was captured by the CPVA on January 4, 1951, but a resurgent UNC recaptured the city for a second time on March 15. By mid-1951, the front lines had become static, running from the Imjin estuary on the west coast to Kansong on the east coast. After a year of fighting, the boundary between North and South Korean territory ran close to where it had been before the war; this remained the case for the rest of the conflict.

The role of air power

Almost from the start, air power played a critical role in the UNC conduct of the war. After the surprise attack by the KPA, it was chiefly US aircraft that slowed the KPA sufficiently for US ground reinforcements to arrive in Korea. Thereafter, UNC ground forces were strongly supported by aircraft and the air forces (including naval aircraft) themselves took the war into North Korea, attacking industrial and military targets, including the transport infrastructure and power-generation system. UNC commanders hoped that the employment of overwhelming air power would indirectly bring about the collapse of the KPA and CPVA. One characteristic of the air war was that, perhaps because of the concentrated area of operations, the differentiation between strategic and tactical tasks was somewhat blurred, particularly in relation to the interdiction mission. The UNC strategic air campaign was also severely limited by political constraints in that the supply facilities in Manchuria remained off limits to attack, despite their being the source of almost all the materiel needed by the KPA and CPVA.

Just as Korea's geographic position affected its political history, so its internal geography and its climate directly influenced conduct of the air campaign. Most of the country is mountainous, particularly in the north, with terrain reaching around 5,000–6,000ft above sea level, but there is lower ground on the western reaches of the peninsula. The weather in the region is dictated by the northerly and southerly monsoons. The former occurs in the winter months and is characterized by extremely cold, but very clear, air. Ground temperatures of -10° centigrade are not unusual and there is frequently a strong northwesterly jet-stream of up to 200 knots at around 30,000ft. The period between October and March is, then, ideal flying weather. However, in the summer months the weather over the Korean peninsula is affected by the southerly monsoon, which brings with it much warmer temperatures (20–30° centigrade), but also thick clouds, heavy prolonged rainfall and thunderstorms, all of which limit aerial activity.

The major industrial centres in Korea were situated in the north of the country, which also benefitted from a hydroelectrical power network which had been constructed by the Japanese. Huge investment by the Japanese in the 1930s had resulted in the establishment of heavy industry, and by the 1940s, Korea was the second most industrialized economy in southeast Asia, after Japan itself. Importantly, Korean armaments factories had been major suppliers to the Japanese forces during World War II. However, wartime damage and subsequent communist mismanagement had left the industrial infrastructure in the North in a very poor state, and by 1950 North Korea had almost reverted to being an agrarian economy, with a populace living at subsistence level. During their occupation, the Japanese had also built an extensive transportation infrastructure, primarily for the movement of military supplies and personnel. Because of its original strategic military purpose, the railway system was designed to be more robust than a typical civilian network of the day. Embankments and cuttings were strongly reinforced, and where bridges and tunnels were built for double track lines, they were often separate structures, sited far enough apart that an attack on one line would not compromise the other. The major railway network

A Soviet-built T-34 tank of the KPA which was disabled by napalm during an airstrike. Air attacks proved to be the most effective way of stopping KPA armored assaults during the first days after the invasion. (US National Archive)

Like all the Japanese-built bridges in Korea, those over the Han River at Seoul were very strongly constructed and proved to be difficult targets to bomb. (US National Archive)

in Korea formed an 'H', with Seoul and Wonsan lying at the cross arm and the others reaching from Sinuiju near the border with Manchuria in the northwest to Mokpo in the southwest, and from Rajin near the border with Russia in the northeast to Pusan in the southeast. From this framework, branch lines extended to other centres, often running along the bottoms of steep-sided valleys as they wove their way through the high ground. The roads in Korea followed a similar pattern to the railway system. They were generally of poor quality in comparison to the railways, but nevertheless provided viable routes for heavy transport vehicles to move across the country.

Despite its dilapidated state, the North Korean industrial base offered worthwhile and vulnerable targets for bombers that would be easy to find and straightforward to attack; in contrast, the road and rail network was a complex lattice in which supplies and personnel could be efficiently moved and easily hidden. The numerous tunnels, which were ideal as shelters and temporary barracks or supply dumps, were also impervious to bombs. The most vulnerable points of the transport system were the many bridges spanning numerous east–west-flowing rivers. However, while bridges could in theory be attacked from the air with relative ease, the practicality of damaging or destroying these rugged structures was a much more difficult task. They were far smaller than industrial sites so bombing had to be far more accurate, and despite their relatively small size they were very strongly constructed. Furthermore, the rivers were shallow and had rocky beds, so they could often be forded in the summer months, while in the winter, the water froze and the ice was thick enough to support vehicular traffic and pedestrians. Thus, simply dropping a span from a bridge would not necessarily stop the flow of traffic. The UNC air forces were to find that the air interdiction of this complicated transport system would be a challenging task.

During the Korean War, the role of UNC air power was threefold: to disable the North Korean war-fighting capability, to interdict supplies and reinforcements before they could reach the front, and to support ground troops in combat. The first of these roles is clearly strategic and the last is clearly tactical, but the interdiction role straddled both definitions.

CHRONOLOGY

1950

June 25 North Korean forces cross the 38th Parallel and invade South Korea

June 27 First mission by 19th BG B-29s over Korea to bomb railway yards at Seoul

June 28 Seoul falls to the Korean People's Army (KPA)

July 1 First B-29 bombing attack on the bridges over the Han River at Seoul

July 8 Far East Air Force (FEAF) Bomber Command formed under command of Maj Gen Emmett O'Donnell

July 8 22nd and 92nd BGs deploy to Japan from USA

July 13 22nd and 92nd BGs fly first mission over Korea to bomb marshalling yards at Wonsan

July 18 Flying from USS *Valley Forge*, CVG-5 bombs the Wonsan oil refinery

July 22 FEAF Target Selection Committee established

July 31 JCS authorizes commencement of strategic bombing

August 1 307th BG deploys to Japan from USA

August 5 98th BG deploys to Japan from USA

August 7 98th BG flies first operational mission to bomb marshalling yards at Pyongyang

August 8 307th BG flies first operational mission, also against marshalling yards at Pyongyang

August 20 Attacks by CVG-11 and 19th BG against the last bridge over the Han River at Seoul

August 23 First RAZON attack by 19th BG

September 15 UNC carries out amphibious landings at Inchon

September 26 92nd BG bombs the Fusen (Pujon) hydroelectric power-generating plant

September 27 Seoul falls to UNC forces

October 22 22nd and 92nd BGs stood down and return to USA

October 25 Chinese People's Volunteer Army (CPVA) enters the conflict

October 26 South Korean troops reach the Yalu River

November 1 First MiG-15 mission of conflict

November 8 B-29s bomb the Sinuiju bridges over the Yalu River

November 9 First B-29 shot down by MiG-15s

November 12 Successful strike by naval aircraft against Sinuiju road bridge

November 25 CPVA offensive opens

1951

January 4 Seoul falls to KPA

January 13 Successful TARZON attack on bridge at Kanggye

January 23 F-84s of 27th FEG strike Sinuiju airfield

March 1 Ten of 18 B-29s severely damaged by MiG-15s while bombing the bridge over the Yalu River at Kogunyong (Cheonggang)

March 2–April 2 Battle of Carlson's Canyon

March UNC counteroffensive, Operation *Ripper*, commences

March 15 Seoul falls to UNC forces

March 29 Unsuccessful TARZON attack on Sinuiju bridges

April 12 B-29 raid against the Sinuiju bridge over the Yalu River; B-29s switch to night operations

May 1 Skyraiders from CVG-19 flying from USS *Princeton* hit Hwachon Dam

June 10 Lt Gen Otto P. Weyland assumes command of FEAF

July 10 First negotiations towards Armistice at Kaesong

August 18 Operation *Strangle* commences

October 13 Shoran-directed night attack on Saamchan airfield

October 18 Daylight raid by 19th BG against Saamchan airfield

October 23 'Black Tuesday', B-29 raid by 307th BG on Namsi airfield, suffers heavy losses to MiG-15s

October 29 Kapsan 'decapitation raid': aircraft from USS *Essex* and *Antietam* bomb communist leadership meeting

1952

January 26– March 11 Campaign against the Wadong Chokepoint

March 3 UNC Operation *Saturate* commences

May 7 Vice Adm Joseph J. 'Jocko' Clark assumes command of 7th Fleet

May 30 Lt Gen Glenn O. Barcus assumes command of 5th AF

June 23 Massed strikes on North Korean hydroelectric power system by carrier-borne and land-based tactical aircraft

July 4 70 fighter-bombers attack the North Korean military academy at Sakchu

July 11 UNC Operation *Pressure Pump* massed strikes against targets in Pyongyang area

July 30 Largest strategic night-bomber raid of the war, 63 B-29s bomb the Oriental Light Metal Company in Sinuiju

August 29 UNC Operation *Pressure Pump 2*, more massed strikes against targets in Pyongyang area

September 1 Largest naval strike of the war, aircraft from USS *Essex* and *Princeton* attack Aoji

September 9 82 F-84s carry out second attack on North Korean military academy at Sakchu

September 15 24 F-84s from the 58th FBG attack the port and supply depot at Sinuiju

September 30 Night raid by 45 B-29s against the Namsan-ni chemical plant

October 8 Joint raid by B-29s and Banshees from VF-11 against rail junction at Kowon (Gowon)

November 8 First night kill of a MiG-15 achieved by Skyknight from VMF(N)-513

1953

January 9–15 Campaign against the Yongmidong and Sinanju bridges

January 29 Last B-29 loss of the war

May 13–22 F-84s attack North Korean irrigation dams

June 10–July 27 Attacks to neutralize North Korean airfields

July 27 Armistice ceasefire declared

ATTACKER'S CAPABILITIES
UN air power

In July 1950, the US Far East Air Force (FEAF), with its headquarters in Japan, was commanded by Lt Gen George E. Stratemeyer, a veteran of the Southeast Asian campaign of World War II. Its main role was the defence of Japan, and its area of responsibility stretched 3,000 miles from the Philippines to Japan, extending southeastwards another 1,500 miles to Guam. The main strength of FEAF was concentrated in the 5th Air Force (5th AF), also based in Japan, under the command of Lt Gen Earle E. Partridge. The 5th AF, whose area of responsibility included Korea, comprised two light bomber squadrons of North American B-26 Invaders of the 3rd Bombardment Group (Light) – BG(L) – and three Lockheed F-80 Shooting Star-equipped Fighter Groups, the 8th Fighter Bomber Group (FBG), the 35th Fighter Interceptor Group (FIG) and the 49th FBG. In addition to these forces, the 13th AF provided some strategic bombing capability with the two Boeing B-29 Superfortress squadrons of the 19th Bombardment Group (BG), which were based on Guam, as well as a further F-80 Group, the 18th FBG, based in the Philippines. A fifth F-80 Group, the 51st FIG, operated from Okinawa under the auspices of the 20th AF.

The surprise attack on South Korea by the KPA found the US and allied forces in the region completely unprepared for a military campaign on the peninsula. The fighter groups had only recently converted from the North American F-51 Mustang to the F-80 and had not yet practiced ground-attack techniques. Furthermore, the B-26s of the 3rd BG(L) were in a poor condition because of a shortage of spare parts. The short-range F-80 was not well suited to missions involving the relatively long transit from Japan to Korea, and the B-29s faced a round-trip distance of some 4,000 miles from Guam to targets near Seoul, well beyond their tactical range. To rectify the former problem, some F-80 units were converted back to the longer-range F-51; meanwhile, the latter problem was addressed by moving the 19th BG to Kadena, on the island of Okinawa, 1,000 miles nearer to the target area.

Within days of the invasion, and despite their shortcomings, all USAF (United States Air Force) aircraft including the B-29s were concentrated in tactical support of the South Korean

The Douglas F3D Skyknight, operated by the US Marine Corps night-fighter squadron VMF(N)-513, proved its worth as a night escort fighter. (NMNA)

OPPOSITE AIRFIELDS 1950–53

In the first weeks of the war, the US/UNC operated from bases in Japan (and Okinawa) before deploying into South Korea; the aircraft were evacuated back to Japan in August 1950 but started to deploy forward again as UNC forces pushed northwards. However, the bases in Japan and Okinawa continued to be used by UNC heavy bombers. During the entire war, the Soviet and Chinese air forces operated from bases in Manchuria.

and American ground forces which were carrying out a courageous fighting withdrawal southeastward towards Pusan. To its great credit, the USAF overcame huge practical difficulties to deliver the air power that largely slowed the KPA advance until it could be stopped completely. By the end of July, enough US Army troops had been deployed in Korea to hold the KPA at the Pusan perimeter. Meanwhile, USAF reinforcements had rushed to Japan, including four more B-29 groups – the 22nd, 92nd, 98th and 307th BGs – which deployed from the continental USA.

The largest and most powerful heavy bomber produced in World War II, the B-29 Superfortress, was already obsolescent by the outbreak of the Korean War and had been reclassified as a 'medium bomber'. Nevertheless, in 1950 it still constituted a powerful striking force: powered by four 2,200hp Wright R-3350-23 Cyclone engines, the B-29 had an operational ceiling of 33,600ft (9,700m) and a combat range of 3,250 miles (5,230km). It could carry up to 20,000lb (9,000kg) of bombs internally. USAF bombers were organized in Groups, each normally composed of three squadrons of 15–20 aircraft. Despite the age of their mounts, B-29 crews were well trained and could achieve good bombing accuracy. While the Pacific-based crews of the 19th BG relied on visual bombing using the Norden bombsight, those based in the continental USA (the 22nd and 92nd BGs) were equipped with the AN/APQ-13 radar which gave them a 'blind bombing' capability. This equipment

The Douglas B-26 Invader (not to be confused with the Martin B-26 Marauder of World War II) was used by 5th AF for day and night interdiction. Later in the conflict, B-26s carried out defence-suppression support for B-29 night raids. (US National Archive)

USSR

CHINA

Mukden

Liaoyang

Anshan

Antung

Tatungkao

Pyongyang

Wonsan

KOREA

Sea of Japan

Yellow
Sea

Kimpo K14   Seoul

Suwon K13

Pyongtaek K6   Osan-ri K55

Pohang K3

Taegu K2

Pusan
Busan

JAPAN

Johnson AB

Yokota AB

Itazuke AB

Okinawa
Kadena AB

US/UNC airfields
Soviet/Chinese airfields
Demarcation Line June 25 1950
Front Lines September 14 1950
Front Lines 25 November 1950
Armistice Line July 27 1953

N

0   100 miles

0   100km

was a development of the World War II-vintage British H2X 3cm radar, which in practice was really only effective for finding coastal or estuarine targets. It was fortunate that most of the strategic targets in North Korea were situated close to the coast or on one of the wide estuaries that punctuated the west coast.

Even without having to deal with target defences, B-29 crews faced a number of challenges from the climate in Korea. During the winter months, the strong jet streams blowing across northern Korea could generate heavy crosswinds, affecting bomb fall and weapon aiming. During the summer, the southerly monsoon brought heavy storm clouds which made visual target acquisition difficult, hence the need for a radar-directed bombing capability. Depending on the expected weather conditions over the target, Superfortress crews used three different bombing tactics. If the weather was good enough for visual target acquisition, they would fly in 'vics' of three aircraft, with wingmen dropping their bombs on the command of the element leader, who aimed visually using the Norden bombsight. If low cloud covered the target, the 'vic' formations would also drop on the command of the element leader, but, in this case, the leader would drop radar-aimed bombs using the AN/APQ-13 equipment. The final tactic, known as 'Hometown,' was used when higher-level cloud precluded formation flying: in this case, the bombers would fly in a one-minute stream and aim their bombs individually by radar.

Another bombing aid, which was to come into its own late in 1951 when the B-29s moved almost exclusively to night bombing, was the SHOrt-RANge (SHORAN) system. Unlike the AN/APQ-13, which was limited to targets close to the coastline, SHORAN could be used over the whole of North Korea. The constituent parts of SHORAN were two AN/APN-2 ground station beacons which fed range and azimuth information to an AN/APN-3 transceiver mounted in the aircraft. The bomber crew followed a range arc from one beacon and released their weapons when they intercepted the azimuth signal from the second beacon. One SHORAN beacon was first sited on South Mountain (Namsan), Seoul, and the other on Tokchok-To (Deokjeokdo) island to the west of Inchon. The

The heaviest bomber of World War II, the Boeing B-29 Superfortress, was obsolescent and had been reclassified as a medium bomber by the outbreak of the Korean War. (US National Archive)

Developed during World War II, the Norden bombsight enabled B-29 bombardiers to aim their weapons visually with great precision. (© Corbis via Getty Images)

system was first in use between November 12 and December 17, 1950, but the results were disappointing because of the poor condition of the beacons and inadequate training of the beacon crews. The beacons were withdrawn in December 1950, but redeployed in early 1951 after further training of the crews and maintenance of the equipment. During this second deployment, four beacon sites were established, two (Able and Charlie sites) on the offshore islands in the Yellow Sea and two (Baker and Dog sites) on mountains close to the 38th Parallel. This time SHORAN proved to be more reliable, and in ideal conditions it would eventually produce an accuracy of 485ft Circular Error Probable (CEP). However, there were still a number of practical problems with using SHORAN in Korea that had to be overcome. Firstly, the navigational precision of the system depended on it having an accurately plotted position for the target, so it was limited to some extent by the inexact mapping coverage of North Korea. Secondly, at longer ranges, the bombers had to fly higher in order to receive the SHORAN signal, with a commensurate reduction in their bombing accuracy. Finally, the B-29 crews in Japan were not familiar with the SHORAN equipment and techniques, having only about eight practices before flying operational missions, whereas it was reckoned that many crews needed as many as 35 sorties to become proficient. Thus, the initial night-bombing operations in November 1951 produced a CEP of 1,220ft. All B-29 crews were given further SHORAN training, but the problem was only properly resolved in the summer of 1952 when experienced SHORAN-qualified replacement crews from the 90th Strategic Reconnaissance Wing began to arrive in theatre. Another drawback with SHORAN was that the transceiver interfered with the Electronic Counter Measures (ECM) equipment carried on the aircraft, so the ECM had to be switched off during the bombing run, making the bomber vulnerable to antiaircraft fire at the most critical part of the mission. Nevertheless, SHORAN techniques were used by the B-29 force, particularly during night operations, with growing success up until the ceasefire in 1953.

With few other strategic targets in North Korea, one of the first tasks of the B-29 force was to destroy the bridges over the large rivers that crossed the main supply routes being

The 1,000lb VB-3 RAnge and AZimuy ONly (RAZON) radio-guided bomb proved the viability of precision-guided munitions in combat, but also highlighted some of the practical problems in using them. (NMUSAF)

used to resupply the KPA. During the Japanese occupation of Korea in the first half of the 20th century, numerous bridges were built to carry road and rail routes across wide reaches of the Yalu, Chongchon, Taedong, Imjin and Han Rivers. These rivers ran east–west into the Yellow Sea, effectively cutting all north–south routes. The bridges crossing them had been constructed to military specifications and were particularly strongly built. In any case, bridges are notoriously difficult targets to hit since they are relatively slender (some Korean bridges were just 8ft wide) and need a direct hit on the structure to do any damage. Although the B-29 crews were capable of remarkably accurate bombing of relatively large targets such as industrial facilities, marshalling yards or military emplacements, hitting bridges was to prove a challenge. Even when direct hits were obtained, there was often little damage to the bridge structure itself. Only the aircraft of the 19th BG had the bomb racks required to carry the 2,000lb bombs necessary to destroy the larger metal bridges, rather than the 500lb or 1,000lb bombs carried by the other groups. Even early in the campaign, before the Antiaircraft Artillery (AAA) defences had been established, FEAF reckoned that more than 13 bomb runs were required to destroy one bridge. The best results were obtained by bombing from 10,000ft at an angle of 40° to the axis of the bridge, but this altitude was no longer feasible once the KPA deployed AAA guns to defend key bridges. For bombers attacking the strategically important bridges over the Yalu River, there was an added complication that they were not permitted to fly north of the river – in other words, they were prohibited from infringing Chinese airspace. Thus, they were constrained to attacking the bridges at 90° to the axis, making these bridges very difficult to hit.

One method of increasing the weapons efficiency was to use guided weapons – specifically the 1,000lb VB-3 RAnge and AZimuy ONly (RAZON) and the 12,000lb VB-13 TAllboy RaZON (TARZON). Developed during World War II, RAZON comprised a 1,000lb bomb fitted with moveable control surfaces in the tail unit, which were activated by radio commands from the bomb aimers. Watching a flare in the tail of the bomb through the bombsight, the bombardier controlled the bomb in range and azimuth by means of a joystick and a radio link to the weapon. Initial RAZON drops by the 19th BG were not particularly accurate, due in the main to the deteriorated condition of control assemblies. However, once this problem had been resolved, the accuracy increased dramatically: between September 29 and October 8, 1950, 179 RAZONs were dropped, of which 120 were classed as satisfactory, a success rate of 67 percent. Control failures did still occur quite regularly, but by the time the last 150 RAZONs had been dropped in December, the success rate for those weapons had risen to 96 percent. The overall results for nearly 500 RAZONs dropped in combat were that over 330 hit their targets. Meanwhile, the 19th BG had commenced operations with the larger TARZON bomb, which promised to be an even better weapon against bridges. Based on the British 'Tallboy' bomb, the TARZON was so large that it did not fit into the B-29 bomb bay and was carried semi-recessed under the fuselage. The delivery profile and guidance system for the weapon were very similar to RAZON and like RAZON, TARZON suffered from early teething problems in Korea. The first four TARZON missions resulted in failure, and of ten TARZONs dropped in December 1950, only one scored a hit. There were some spectacular successes, including the destruction of a bridge at Kanggye on January 13, 1951, but of a total of 30 TARZONs dropped in combat, only seven hit their targets. Although the accuracy of crews dropping TARZONs had been improving dramatically with practice, use of the weapon was discontinued after the loss of a B-29 which jettisoned a TARZON after losing two engines due to battle damage on April 29, 1951: it was discovered that despite being jettisoned 'safe,' at low level the TARZON would detonate on contact with the surface beneath the aircraft, with disastrous results for the bomber.

In the first months of the conflict, B-29s were virtually unopposed during daylight raids; in their few encounters, the Korean People's Air Force Yak-9Ps posed little threat to the bombers. However, the introduction of heavy-calibre AAA guns and Soviet MiG-15 fighters from December 1950 changed the situation completely. The bombers were thereafter forced to bomb from higher altitudes to avoid the AAA, affecting their accuracy, and escort fighters were needed to defend the bombers from Soviet interceptors. During daylight raids, the bombers flew in formations of up to 50 aircraft, made up of sections of three or four aircraft, each giving the others cross-cover from their ten 0.5in machine guns. These tactics had proven successful against the propellor-driven fighters

A 12,000lb VB-13 TAllboy RaZON (TARZON) weapon is loaded into a specially adapted B-29. A small number of B-29s were modified to carry the TARZON over Korea. (US National Archive)

RAZON tactics

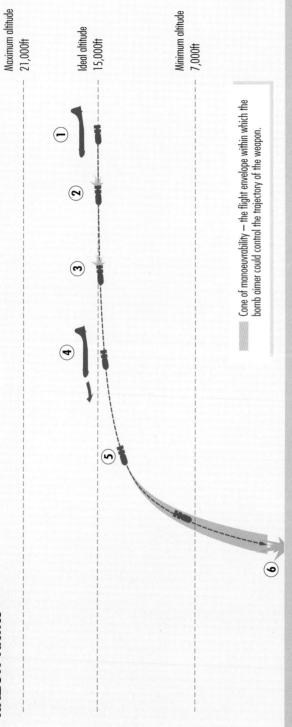

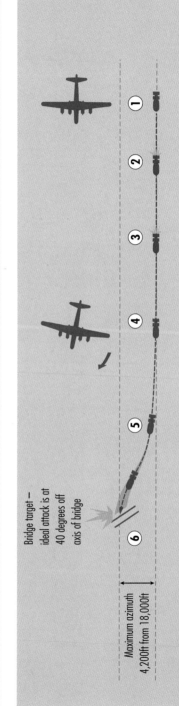

Maximum altitude
21,000ft

Ideal altitude
15,000ft

Minimum altitude
7,000ft

Cone of manoeuvrability – the flight envelope within which the bomb aimer could control the trajectory of the weapon.

Bridge target – ideal attack is at 40 degrees off axis of bridge

Maximum azimuth 4,200ft from 18,000ft

1. Bomb dropped
2. 1,000,000 candlepower flare ignites, radio contact established with bomber
3. Flare captured in 'Crab' and projected onto target image
4. Post-release, bomber can turn 15 degrees away using maximum 8 degrees bank
5. Bomb aimer controls bomb in range and azimuth
6. 'Jag' factors control inputs to allow for new time of fall

of World War II, but crews found to their cost that they were not as effective against the MiG-15. In late 1951, the ferocity of attacks by MiG-15s forced the B-29s to switch to night bombing, using SHORAN to locate their targets. At first, the bombers found themselves unopposed once more, but the North Korean defences soon caught up. On clear nights, contrails, which would often form above 20,000ft, could pinpoint the exact position of bombers, so crews learnt to avoid the contrail levels; blackpainted undersides were also surprisingly successful in concealing the aircraft from searchlights. In addition, from December 1951, the 307th BG started to escort its bombers with aircraft equipped exclusively as radar jammers. These aircraft also dropped 'window' metallic foil to decoy the radars. Another effective tactic was to overwhelm the defences in a compressed attack, with bombers attacking in short time intervals from different attack tracks. From October 1952, the interval between individual bombers during night attacks was reduced from three minutes to just one minute.

However, despite all of these tactics, GCI (Ground-Controlled Intercept)-directed MiG-15 night fighters still proved a serious threat, forcing FEAF to carry out night escort and fighter sweeps by USMC (US Marine Corps) Douglas F3D Skyknight fighters and later USAF Lockheed F-94B Starfires. The most northerly UNC radar station, with the callsign 'Dentist,' which was based on Cho-do island (off the west coast and approximately halfway between Seoul and Pyongyang), could only offer limited coverage of the Yalu River sector; thus, UNC night fighters faced a double challenge in avoiding the bombers and also locating the Soviet night fighters without the aid of accurate GCI. The Skyknight was introduced to Korea in late June 1952 to the resident night-fighter unit, VMF(N)-513. USMC night-fighter crews were well trained, and although VMF(N)-513 was new to the Skyknight, its crews already had considerable night combat experience in theatre flying the Vought F4U-4N Corsair and Grumman F7F Tigercat over Korea. Despite its modest performance, the Skyknight proved to be a very effective night fighter and its AN/APS-28 tail warning radar gave it a particular advantage in alerting the crew to potential counterattacks by MiG-15s. The initial tactic was to set up a Combat Air Patrol (CAP) in an orbit just south of the Yalu River. Two CAPs, one high and one low, were employed to act as a barrier to Soviet and Chinese night fighters crossing from north of the river.

Operated by the 319th FIS, which deployed to Suwon in March 1952, the F-94Bs were not at first permitted to operate north of the front lines, lest the state-of-the-art Hughes E-1 fire control system should fall into enemy hands if an aircraft was shot down. This restriction severely limited the employment of the F-94B, leaving the bulk of the night-fighter sweep and escort duties during the summer and autumn of 1952 to VMF(N)-513 and the Skyknight. The F-94B was eventually released to operate over North Korea in November 1952, when it took over responsibility for the barrier CAPs, typically employing between four and six aircraft each night. This in turn released the Skyknights to fly as close escorts, shadowing the bombers, flying 2,000–3,000ft above them on their route into and out of the target area. This technique enabled the Skyknights to engage MiG-15s which attempted to intercept bombers illuminated by searchlights.

Amongst the first reinforcements to arrive in theatre at the start of the conflict was the aircraft carrier USS *Valley Forge* (CV-45), which had been docked at Subic Bay in the Philippines when the KPA invasion was launched. It would later be joined by other aircraft carriers of the US 7th Fleet, which carried out operational tours as part of Task Force 77 (TF 77), operating predominantly off the east coast of Korea, until the end of hostilities. Each carrier was the home of three fighter squadrons – each equipped with either the F4U

The main strike aircraft of the US Navy carrier fleet was the Douglas AD Skyraider, which took part in numerous strategic attacks as well as meeting interdiction and Close Air Support tasks during the conflict. (NMNA)

Corsair, Grumman F9F Panther or McDonnell F3H Banshee – and an attack squadron flying Douglas AD Skyraiders. The fighter squadrons were soon pressed into service as fighter-bombers, but it was the Skyraiders that gave the carrier air group its striking power. Fitted with a single variant of the same engine as the B-29, the Skyraider could carry a 2,000lb bombload plus air-to-ground rockets over a range of 1,200 miles, or up to 6,500lb of weapons over shorter distances.

Operating predominantly off the eastern coast of Korea and unconstrained by the battle lines, carrier-based aircraft had an almost free rein over northeastern Korea. They were able to attack both strategic and tactical targets, and since they generally operated outside the range of Antung-based MiG-15s, the main danger to them was small-calibre AAA. Since, in the days before angled flight decks, aircraft carriers could either launch or recover aircraft, but could not carry out both operations simultaneously, naval aircraft generally carried out 'deck launches' in which the whole Carrier Air Group (CVG) would take off as one large formation. To counter the threat of AAA to bombers, some of the fighter-bombers would be tasked to attack the target defences either with bombs, rockets, or napalm. Airstrikes by carrier aircraft were very effective, but they were constrained by the weather in the Sea of Japan, where typhoons were not infrequent.

Because of the difficulties in coordination between land- and carrier-based aircraft, the CVGs tended to operate autonomously, mainly carrying out interdiction strikes, but often also flying tactical missions in support of ground troops. Nevertheless, navy aircraft carried out a number of strategic attacks and the Skyraiders of TF 77 also participated in some joint missions with land-based aircraft against strategic targets, including bridges over the Yalu and the North Korean hydroelectric power infrastructure. Like the USAF, the US Navy found bridges to be difficult targets, and typically it took between 12 and 16 Skyraider sorties – each dropping 2,000lb bombs – to take down a structure. Navy pilots and crews were well trained, and although each carrier joined TF 77 for a few months at a time, the overlap between deployments of the various carriers in the fleet enabled operational lessons and wisdom to be shared amongst the ships and CVGs.

In response to the appearance of the MiG-15 in the skies over North Korea, the 27th Fighter Escort Group (FEG) deployed from Bergstrom Air Force Base, Texas, to Korea with its Republic F-84 Thunderjets in November 1950. At the same time, the North American F-86 Sabres of the 4th FIG deployed from Wilmington, Delaware. The intention was to use the F-86s as a fighter sweep ahead of the bomber force, while the F-84s acted as a close fighter escort to engage any MiG-15s that escaped the F-86 screen. Unfortunately, the straight-winged F-84 lacked the performance to counter the swept-wing MiG-15 and proved completely ineffective in its role; however, the aircraft did prove to be ideal as a fighter-bomber. By mid-1951, the F-84 had taken over from the F-80 as the prime ground-attack jet in the UNC inventory in Korea, equipping the 49th and 136th FBGs.

From bases in South Korea such as Suwon, Kimpo and Taegu, the F-84 could reach targets as far north as the Yalu River and could typically carry two 500lb or 1,000lb bombs against strategic targets such as bridges, dams, or military installations; the aircraft also flew battlefield support and interdiction missions, armed with bombs, rockets, and napalm. The aircraft was equipped with the A-1C(M) computing gunsight, which was optimized for air-to-air firing but could be used in a depressed mode for bombing. However, pilots found that it was not particularly accurate in the 'automatic' mode and instead caged the sight during weapon delivery passes. The results in 'caged' mode were much better:

Perhaps the most glamorous aircraft type to participate in the Korean War, the North American F-86 Sabre proved to be a match for the MiG-15 and was exceptionally well suited to the air superiority role. (US National Archive)

A flight of three Republic F-84E Thunderjets of the 27th FEG, which deployed to Korea in late November 1950 to act as fighter escort to bomber aircraft. Unfortunately, the straight-wing F-84 was no match for the swept-wing MiG-15 in air-to-air combat and it was soon switched to the ground-attack role. The aircraft nearest the camera was shot down by antiaircraft fire near Sinanju on October 13, 1951. (NMUSAF)

a CEP of 25ft could be achieved, rather than the 185ft of the automatic mode. In mid-1951, a typical F-84 attack profile was from a 20° dive from 8,000ft, releasing at 1,200ft at 460mph. This technique was accurate and also minimized the exposure to antiaircraft fire, although AAA guns remained the most serious threat to fighter-bomber operations. In the six months from August 1951 to January 1952, F-84s flew 16,753 sorties and only seven aircraft were lost to enemy fighters, whereas AAA fire accounted for a further 32. The F-84 dive-bombing profile was developed further by the 49th FBG in mid-1952 into a 45° dive from 11,000ft, giving a release between 9,000 and 7,500ft, thus generating a better stand-off from AAA defences. When operating against airfields, the aim was to cut the operating strip into lengths of less than 3,000ft, which was thought to be the minimum take-off distance for the MiG-15.

UNC fighter-bomber pilots (from the USA, Australia and South Africa) were well trained and well organized. Rather than whole units rotating through Korea, pilots were posted individually to Korea for a tour of 100 operational sorties. The advantage of this system was that there was a continuous but gradual turnover of personnel, enabling the more experienced pilots to pass on the lessons that they and their predecessors had learnt to the less experienced pilots. Upon arrival in Korea, newly arrived pilots attended a short 'Clobber College' where they learnt the procedures for operating in Korea, were shown how to manoeuvre their aircraft hard in combat, and were taught how the search and rescue system worked. It was undoubtedly a major morale boost to pilots to know that a comprehensive search and rescue organization was on hand if they were shot down. Regardless of their seniority, the new pilots would fly their early missions as wingmen, progressing to flight lead status after they had proved their competence in combat. The F-84 groups generally operated in four-aircraft flights, which sometimes operated autonomously and sometimes made up much larger formations of perhaps 60 aircraft.

The attacking forces available to the UNC for attacking strategic targets were large, and although they varied in composition, their aircrews were professional and disciplined. The mix of large bombers, high-performance fighter-bombers, and carrier-based aircraft gave great flexibility and, with SHORAN, an all-weather and night capability.

DEFENDER'S CAPABILITIES
Air defence in North Korea

The North Korean invasion was supported by the Korean People's Air Force (KPAF), which comprised a regiment of Il-10 Sturmovik ground-attack aircraft and a regiment of Yak-9P fighters. However, after quickly destroying the South Koreans' Republic of Korea Air Force (ROKAF), which comprised only a handful of light aircraft, the KPAF was itself soon overwhelmed by the massive force of the UNC. The KPAF was rebuilt over the next two years, but it played little part in defensive air operations over Korea, which were fought chiefly by the Chinese People's Liberation Army Air Force (PLAAF) and the Soviet Voyenno-Vozdushnye Sily (VVS).

The PLAAF had been formed in 1949 under the command of General Liu Yalou, largely in response to air raids on Shanghai carried out by the Nationalist Chinese bombers based in Taiwan. The nascent air force was equipped and trained by the USSR and was still in the early stages of build-up and training at the outbreak of the Korean War. There were no combat-ready pilots in the PLAAF; in any case, at that stage the campaign in Korea seemed to have little relevance to China. The situation changed dramatically after UNC forces advanced to the Manchurian border on the Yalu River in October 1950, triggering the intervention of the CPVA led by Marshal Peng Dehuai. Since the PLAAF was not yet capable of securing Chinese airspace against possible US attack, the responsibility was taken on by the VVS, which also undertook to defend the bridges over the Yalu River at Antung (now Dandong) and the hydroelectric plant at the Suiho (now Supung) dam, as well as lines of communication and industrial facilities in Korea as far south as a line between Pyongyang and Wonsan.

The Soviet fighter units were equipped with the Mikoyan-Gurevich MiG-15 jet fighter, which, thanks to its swept wings and Klimov KV-1 engine (an improved version of the Rolls Royce Nene), enjoyed arguably the highest performance of any fighter aeroplane at the time. It was closely matched by the F-86 Sabre but had a better ceiling (by 5,000–6,000ft) and a better rate of climb above about 20,000ft than the American aircraft. Both types were roughly comparable in turning performance above 30,000ft, but the Sabre turned slightly

MiG-15s of the 29th GvIAP at Dachang airfield in April 1950, well before the deployment of Soviet fighter regiments to Korea. The introduction of the MiG-15 over Korea signaled the end of UN air supremacy over North Korea. (Krylov & Tepsurkaev)

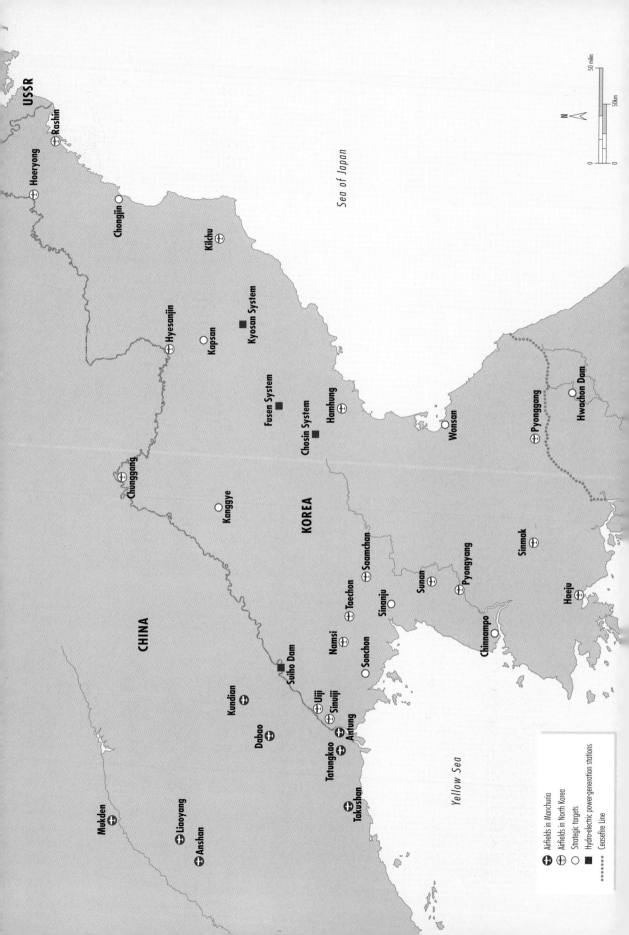

USSR

Rashin

Hoeryong

Chongjin

Kilchu

Sea of Japan

Hyesanjin

Kapsan

Kyosan System

Fusen System

Chosin System

Hamhung

Wonsan

Pyonggang

Hwachon Dam

Chunggang

Kanggye

KOREA

Sinmak

CHINA

Saamchon

Sunan

Pyongyang

Haeju

Taechon

Sinanju

Namsi

Suiho Dam

Sonchon

Chinnampo

Kundian

Uiji

Sinuiji

Dabao

Tatungkao

Antung

Yellow Sea

Takushan

Mukden

Liaoyang

Anshan

50 miles

50 km

N

Airfields in Manchuria
Airfields in North Korea
Strategic targets
Hydro-electric power-generation stations
Ceasefire Line

OPPOSITE AIRFIELDS AND MAJOR TARGETS IN NORTH KOREA

During the Korean War, Soviet and Chinese MiG-15s flew from airfields in Manchuria. Throughout the conflict, a programme of building new airfields in North Korea continued – and these airfields were targeted by UNC bombers. The other strategic targets marked on the map, including the power-generating stations at the Suiho Dam and the Chosin, Fusen and Kyosan hydro-electric systems, were also attacked by UNC aircraft.

better than the MiG below that altitude. However, the MiG-15 had not been designed as an air superiority fighter, but as a bomber destroyer: its armament of two 23mm Nudelman-Richter NR-23 cannons and one 37mm Nudelman N-37 cannon was intended to pack enough punch to disable a B-29. Thus, the introduction of the MiG-15 into the skies over North Korea in late 1950 posed a significant threat to FEAF strategic bomber operations.

Liu Yalou, chief of the Chinese People's Liberation Army Air Force (CPLAAF) from its formation in 1949, oversaw the service as it grew into a large combat-experienced air force. (author)

A MiG-15 of the Korean People's Air Force (KPAF). The MiG-15 was arguably the best fighter aeroplane of its day, a rugged machine with a higher ceiling and better rate of climb than the North American F-86 Sabre. (US National Archive)

Like the USA, the USSR and China feared the consequences of the war spreading beyond Korea, and all sides went to great lengths to ensure that it did not do so. In particular, the Soviet involvement in the war was kept secret. Soviet pilots entered China dressed in Chinese uniforms, carrying nothing that could identify themselves as Russian, and their aircraft were painted with North Korean markings. At first, the Soviets were instructed to use only pre-learnt Korean phrases over the radio, but this policy was soon abandoned after it proved unworkable in combat. Soviet pilots were forbidden to fly over water (in case they were shot down and subsequently picked up by the UNC naval forces), and nor were they to fly south of the Pyongyang–Wonsan line (although this was largely impossible because of the limited range of the MiG-15). On the other hand, they were aware that UNC pilots were prohibited from flying into Chinese airspace north of the Yalu River, so they enjoyed a sanctuary in which to prepare for battle or to withdraw to if the tactical situation was unfavourable.

Soviet Istrebitel'naya Aviatsionnaya Diviziya (IAD, Fighter Aviation Divisions) were typically made up of three *Istrebitel'naya Aviatsionnaya Polk* (IAP, Fighter Aviation Regiments), each in turn comprising three squadrons of about 18–20 aircraft. The first units of the Soviet 151st IAD deployed to China in late October 1950: the 72nd Guards IAP (GvIAP) were based at Mukden North (now Shenyang), 28th Fighter Regiment (IAP) at Anshan, and the 139th GvIAP at Liaoyang. A second fighter division, the 28th IAD, comprising the 139th GvIAP (transferred from the 151st IAD) and 67th IAP, was formed at Liaoyang in early November. It was followed on November 20 by the 50th IAD, comprising the 29th and 177th IAPs, at Anshan. Initially, much of the tasking for these units was the training of PLAAF pilots, leaving only one fighter division to cover the air defence task. On November 27, the three Soviet IADs were formed into the 64th Fighter Corps (IAK), under the command of Maj

Gen I. V. Belov. Soviet MiG-15 pilots were experienced and capable fighter pilots, many of whom had distinguished combat records from World War II.

The three original bases were about 100 miles to the northwest of Antung, so the fighters needed to carry external fuel drop tanks to give them the necessary tactical range to patrol over the Korean border. During December 1950, the 50th IAD moved its MiG-15 operation forward to Antung to enable its pilots to react more quickly to UNC raids. Standing patrols by aircraft flying from the Mukden–Liaoyang–Anshan area could still provide a degree of 'top cover' or carry out diversionary attacks against UNC escort fighters while the Antung-based fighters climbed to altitude. After receiving radar warning that UNC formations were heading northwards, the MiG-15s could take off and climb in the 'safe' airspace north of the Yalu before entering Korean airspace under GCI direction to intercept the attackers. Since the combats occurred close to overhead their base, the MiGs could use almost all of their fuel while engaged without having to worry about a long

Maj Gen Ivan V. Belov commanded the Soviet 64th IAK between November 1950 and September 1951. (Igor Seidov)

A Soviet P-35 (NATO codename Bar Lock) early warning and intercept control radar, which was developed from the P-20 Periskop used by the Soviets in Manchuria during the Korean War. The P-20 was very similar in appearance to the P-35. (US National Archive)

transit home. Similarly, any aircraft that were damaged in combat could dive quickly to the safety of the Antung runway. Other bases were built in the area over the course of the war: nicknamed the 'Antung Complex' by UNC pilots, the airfields included Tatungkao (known to the Soviets as Miaoergou) from May 1951, Takushan from October 1951, Dabao (known to Soviet pilots as Dapu and to UNC pilots as Fengchen) from July 1952, and Kuandian from November 1952.

Unlike the USAF system of 'roulement' of pilots through individual combat tours in Korea, the Soviets replaced complete regiments after operational deployments of between six and nine months. Thus, the 151st, 50th and 28th IADs were replaced wholesale by the fresh 324th and 303rd IADs in April/May 1951. This approach had advantages in terms of unit cohesion, but it meant that each new unit had to relearn many of the tactical lessons that had already been learned in combat by its predecessor. Indeed, UNC pilots remarked on the cyclical nature of the ability and aggression shown by MiG-15 pilots.

Both the PLAAF and the KPAF, which were amalgamated into the Unified Air Army (UAA) in March 1951, employed the same system of rotating units through combat tours. Since the PLAAF was still building up from a standing start just two years previously, PLAAF fighter divisions consisted only of two regiments, rather than the three of the equivalent Soviet units. The first PLAAF regiments, the 7th and 10th Fighter Regiments, began operations in early 1951. The Chinese enjoyed some success against UNC bombers, but the inexperience of these barely trained pilots made them more of a liability than an asset, and after a few months they were withdrawn from the front line. PLAAF units returned to the fray in September 1951, although, once again, their effectiveness was limited at first by their lack of experience.

During early 1951, Soviet MiG-15s tended to operate in sections of six to eight aircraft, sometimes operating as an autonomous flight and at other times coordinated with two more sections as part of a larger regimental formation. As the combats developed through the year, the MiG-15 formations became bigger and from the summer, UNC raids would often be met by division-sized formations of 40-plus aircraft. One regimental formation of around 20 aircraft might tie up the escort fighters, while the remaining MiGs attacked the bombers. These tactics proved to be very effective against B-29s and by the autumn of 1951, the Superfortresses had been forced to operate by night.

In 1951, the Soviets also trialled the tactic of using their own aircraft to attack escort fighters, leaving PLAAF aircraft to attack fighter-bombers. The main obstacle to the successful coordination of Soviet and Chinese units was that of language, with Chinese pilots unable to understand the instructions of Russian GCI controllers. By the end of 1951, the PLAAF had adopted the tactic of flying in large division-sized formations, known to UNC pilots as 'trains,' flying a fixed route from the Suiho dam southwards to Pyongyang and then north to Antung. At first, the Chinese pilots seemed reluctant to engage UNC fighters and fighter-bombers, unless they had a clear advantage, but as their experience and confidence increased, so did their aggression, and their attacks became more frequent and effective. The PLAAF played little part in the defence against B-29 night bombers, but as its strength built up (reaching five fighter divisions by the summer of 1952) it became more important in combating UNC fighter-bombers.

From the winter of 1951–52, the UNC B-29 force was restricted to flying night-time missions over North Korea and the air defences against them had to adapt accordingly. An independent night-fighter regiment, the 351st IAP, began flying from Antung in September

A Soviet 100mm KS-19 antiaircraft gun. In theory, these weapons could reach up to 40,000ft; they presented a considerable threat to propeller-driven bombers like the B-29. (US National Archive)

1951. It was equipped with the Lavochkin La-11, a single-seat fighter powered by a Shvetsov ASh-82FN radial piston engine and armed with three 23mm Nudelman-Suranov NS-23 cannons. Although it enjoyed an impressive turn of speed at lower levels, the La-11 lacked the performance to catch the B-29 and it was soon replaced by the MiG-15. Another specialist MiG-15 night-fighter squadron, from the 147th GvIAP, joined the order of battle flying from Tatungkao in May 1952. During night sorties, pilots were directed towards their targets by GCI, but the pilot had to find his quarry visually, with the help of searchlights or tracer fire from the AAA batteries.

From 1952, the Soviet/UAA air defence system was equipped with various early warning and GCI radar systems, including the Soviet P-3 Pegmantit (NATO codename Dumbo), P-8 Dolfin (Knife Rest A) and P-20 Peryskop (Token) systems. Operating in the S-band, the P-20 radar, which incorporated a height-finding facility, proved to be almost impossible to jam.

As well as fighter aircraft, air defence in North Korea was provided by the AAA units of the CPVA/KPA. By mid-1952, it was estimated that some 1,400 37mm 61-K AAA guns and a further 400 85mm M1939 guns had been deployed in North Korea. The smaller-calibre weapons posed little threat to the B-29s, which operated well above the 4,500ft effective ceiling of the guns, but proved very effective against UNC fighter-bombers; however, the larger cannons could reach up into the B-29 bombing altitudes. In theory, the 85mm guns could engage targets at 25,000ft, but in practice they were not particularly effective against aircraft flying above 18,000ft. By February 1952, FEAF B-29s had flown 8,700 sorties for the loss of only five aircraft to AAA fire. A British scientific report published in June 1952 estimated that for every 1,000 daylight B-29 sorties flown, 28 aircraft would be hit by AAA fire, of which half would be destroyed; however, at night, the hit rate was reduced to only six aircraft per 1,000 sorties. As the war continued, more Chinese and Soviet AAA guns were deployed and by May 1953 there were over 780 large-calibre AAA guns sited in North Korea. Most of these guns were 85mm and 100mm weapons, which were also supported by around 500 searchlights.

Initially, AAA guns were deployed around strategic targets, such as airfields, bridge complexes, and vital stretches of railway. Typically, 85mm batteries contained between four and eight guns, and they were usually deployed in a defensive grouping of about 20 heavy guns supported by some 35 lighter-calibre weapons, but these numbers were increased where targets were vulnerable to UNC fighter-bomber attack. Some strategic targets were particularly heavily defended, including the Suiho dam, which in May 1953 was protected by over 160 large-calibre guns, making it the largest concentration of AAA guns in Korea. Airfields were also particularly well defended until mid-1952, when it became clear that the operating surfaces were indefensible against sustained bomber attack; from that date, AAA guns covered only Pyongyang and Sinuiju airfields, since these guns also defended the other targets around those cities. CPVA/KPA intelligence had also worked out the most likely attack axes against strategic targets if bombers were following SHORAN arcs, and gun batteries were sited, with some success, under these flight paths.

In combat, most of the AAA guns were aimed visually using the Puazo-3 fire control directors coupled with the 4-metre DJa optical rangefinder, or else were fired in a barrage. However, gun-laying radars started to become available in 1951, albeit in relatively small numbers. These included the SON-4 (NATO codename Whiff), a Soviet-built version of the US SCR-584 automatic tracking radar, as well as the British G. L. Mark II. By March 1953, there were 32 gun-laying radars controlling about 220 of the large-calibre weapons. Although the radars improved the accuracy of the guns, they were susceptible to the ECM used by the B-29 force.

The air defences of North Korea proved to be very effective and took their toll of UNC aircraft. The Soviet MiG-15 pilots were successful in driving the B-29s from the daylight skies, but their short range and political constraints meant that they covered only a relatively small operational area. Furthermore, the quality of pilots was very variable, ranging from Soviet World War II veterans to Chinese and North Korean novices. Perhaps the most effective element of the air defence system was the AAA, which shot down proportionally far more UNC bomber aircraft.

Arguably the most important capability of the KPA/CPVA was the ability to repair the damage inflicted by UNC aircraft and to build bypass bridges to ensure that the flow of traffic was virtually unaffected. One example of this was the railway bridge across the Chongchon River at Sinanju, which was destroyed by retreating UNC forces in January 1951. A bypass bridge had been constructed by February 4, and although it was bombed on March 1, it was repaired just three weeks later, by which time a second bypass bridge was already under construction.

ORDERS OF BATTLE		
USAF B-29 Strategic Bomber Units		
19th BG	Kadena AB	June 27, 1950 – July 27, 1953
22nd BG	Kadena AB	July 8, 1950 – October 22, 1950
92nd BG	Yokota AB	July 8, 1950 – October 22, 1950
98th BG	Yokota AB	August 5, 1950 – July 27, 1953
307th BG	Kadena AB	August 1, 1950 – July 27, 1953
USN AD Skyraider Strike Units		
VA-35	USS Leyte (CV-32)	September 6, 1950 – February 1, 1951
VA-45	USS Lake Champlain (CV-39)	April 26, 1953 – December 4, 1953
VA-55	USS Valley Forge (CV-45)	May 1, 1950 – December 1, 1950
	USS Princeton (CV-37)	May 31, 1951 – August 29, 1951
	USS Essex (CV-9)	June 16, 1952 – February 6, 1953
VA-65	USS Boxer (CV-21)	August 24, 1950 – November 11, 1950
	USS Valley Forge	December 8, 1950 – March 2, 1951
	USS Philippine Sea (CV-47)	March 29, 1951 – June 9, 1951
	USS Boxer (CV-21)	February 8, 1952 – September 26, 1952
VA-75	USS Bon Homme Richard (CV-31)	May 20, 1952 – January 8, 1953
VA-95	USS Philippine Sea (CVA-47)	December 15, 1952 – August 14, 1953
VA-115	USS Philippine Sea (CV-47)	July 5, 1950 – March 29, 1951
	USS Valley Forge (CV-45)	March 30, 1951 – April 7, 1951
	USS Philippine Sea (CV-47)	December 31, 1951 – August 8, 1952
VA-155	USS Princeton (CVA-37)	January 24, 1953 – September 21, 1953
VA-194	USS Valley Forge (CV-45)	October 15, 1951 – July 3, 1952
	USS Boxer (CVA-21)	March 30, 1953 – November 28, 1953
VA-195	USS Princeton (CV-37)	November 9, 1950 – May 29, 1951
	USS Princeton (CV-37)	March 21, 1952 – November 3, 1952
VA-702	USS Boxer (CV-21)	March 2, 1951 – October 24, 1951
	USS Kearsarge (CVA-33)	August 11, 1952 – March 17, 1953
VA-728	USS Antietam (CV-36)	September 8, 1951 – May 2, 1952
VA-923	USS Bon Homme Richard (CV-31)	May 10, 1951 – December 17, 1951
	USS Oriskany (CVA-34)	September 15, 1952 – May 18, 1953
VF-54	USS Essex (CV-9)	June 26, 1950 – March 25, 1952
	USS Valley Forge (CVA-45)	November 20, 1952 – June 25, 1953
USAF F-84 Fighter Bomber Units		
27th FEG	Taegu (K-2)	December 5, 1950 – January 30, 1951
	Itazuke AB	January 31, 1951 – July 2, 1951
49th FBG	Taegu (K-2)	September 1951 – July 27, 1953
58th FBG	Taegu (K-2)	July 10, 1952 – July 27, 1953
116th FBG	Taegu (K-2)	November 1951 – June 1952
136th FBG	Itazuke AB	May 1951 – September 1951
	Taegu (K-2)	September 26, 1951 – July 10, 1952
474th FBG	Kunsan (K-8)	July 10, 1952 – July 27, 1953
USAF/USMC Fighter Units		
4th FIG (F-86)	Johnson AB	December 13, 1950 – March 29, 1951
	Suwon (K-13)	March 30, 1951 – August 22, 1951
	Kimpo (K-14)	August 23, 1951 – July 27, 1953

51st FIG (F-86)	Itazuke AB	January 3, 1951 – July 30, 1951
	Suwon (K-13)	July 31, 1951 – July 27, 1953
319th FIS (F-94B)	Suwon (K-13)	March 22, 1952 – July 27, 1953
VMF(N)-513 (Skyknight)	Kunsan (K-8)	June 27, 1952 – July 27, 1953
VVS MiG-15 Units		
151st GvIAD	Mukden/Anshan	November 1, 1950 – November 30, 1950
	Antung	February 6, 1951 – April 2, 1951
28th IAD	Liaoyang	November 1, 1959 – November 30, 1950
50th IAD	Anshan	November 25, 1950 – December 3, 1950
	Antung	December 3, 1950 – February 6, 1951
324th IAD	Antung	April 3, 1951 – January 30, 1952
303rd IAD	Tatungkao	May 1951 – February 20, 1952
97th IAD	Antung	January 25, 1952 – May 13, 1952
	Mukden-West	May 13, 1952 – August 28, 1952
190th IAD	Tatungkao*	February 14, 1952 – August 10, 1952
133rd IAD	Tatungkao*	May 15, 1952 – July 4, 1952
	Mukden-West	July 5, 1952 – January 13, 1953
216th IAD	Tatungkao & Dabao	July 30, 1952 – July 27, 1953
32nd IAD	Mukden-West	August 27, 1952 – January 20, 1953
	Antung & Dabao	January 20, 1953 – July 27, 1953
578th IAP (Pacific Fleet)	Antung	September 26, 1952 – January 23, 1953
	Mukden-West	January 23, 1953 – February 16, 1953
781st IAP (Pacific Fleet)	Tatungkao & Dabao	February 21, 1953 – July 27, 1953
351st IAP (Night Fighter)	Anshan & Antung	September 9, 1951 – February 16, 1953
298th IAP (Night Fighter)	Tatungkao & Antung	February 20, 1953 – July 27, 1953
*also detachments to Anshan, Antung and Dabao		
CPLAAF MiG-15 Units*		
2nd Fighter Div	Antung	December 1951 – January 1952
3rd Fighter Div	Antung	October 1951 – January 1952
	Mukden	January 1952 – May 1952
	Antung	June 1952 – January 1953
4th Fighter Div	Antung	December 1950 – July 1951
	Antung	January 1952 – May 1952
	Mukden	June 1952 – July 1953
6th Fighter Div	Tatungkao	December 1951 – May 1952
	Takushan	June 1952 – December 1952
12th Fighter Div	Takushan	March 1952 – June 1952
	Dabao	July 1952 – November 1952
	Takushan	December 1952 – March 1953
14th Fighter Div	Takushan	November 1951 – February 1952
	Takushan	November 1952 – July 1953
15th Fighter Div	Takushan	January 1952 – May 1952
	Takushan	October 1952 – July 1953
16th Fighter Div	Tatungkao	January 1953 – July 1953
17th Fighter Div	Tatungkao	March 1952 – July 1953
18th Fighter Div	Takushan	May 1952 – December 1952
*the exact dates for these deployments are unknown		

CAMPAIGN OBJECTIVES
Air power in a complex war

During the Korean War, the UNC strategic air operations were not part of a constant and consistent campaign. Rather, shaped by events, personalities and political considerations, they evolved in both scope and purpose over the three years of conflict. In addition, the nature of the conflict in Korea meant that there was significant overlap in targeting between strategic bombing and tactical air interdiction. Initially, the North Korean invasion had taken US commanders completely by surprise, to the extent that there were not even any contingency plans in place to cover such an event. Thus, instead of retaliating with a pre-planned strategic campaign, FEAF was forced into reactive crisis management. With few US troops on the ground in Korea, tactical air power suddenly became the means to slow the KPA advance until sufficient ground forces could be deployed from Japan to halt it. Not until the immediate threat by the KPA had been contained was there sufficient breathing space to plan a coordinated interdiction and strategic bombing campaign.

FEAF operations over Korea were strongly influenced by inter-service rivalry and the personal relationships between the various force commanders. The United States Air Force (USAF) had only been established as an independent service since September 18, 1947, prior to which it had been the US Army Air Force (USAAF), a subordinate arm of the Army. Many Army commanders felt that it should have remained so. At the outset of hostilities, the UNC Commander-in-Chief, Gen Douglas MacArthur, had made it clear to FEAF commander Lt Gen Stratemeyer that he regarded the air defence of Japan as the prime role of FEAF and that for the time being strategic operations were low on his priority list. Furthermore, Lt Gen Edward M. Almond, the deputy C-in-C, still believed that tasking for air operations should be determined solely by Army requirements. Indeed, Almond bypassed the FEAF chain of command and passed his instructions directly to Lt Gen Partridge, the 5th AF commander; staff officers at HQ 5th AF also felt under pressure to answer any call from the Army for tactical air support, regardless of whether or not it was sensible to do so. As a result, B-29 crews sometimes found themselves tasked with Close Air Support (CAS) missions – something for which they were not trained and for which their aircraft type was

Vice-Admiral Arthur D. Struble, commanding USN 7th Fleet, on the left, conferring with the United Nations Command (UNC) deputy Commander-in-Chief, Lt Gen Edward M. Almond. Their relations with FEAF were marred by inter-service prejudice. (US National Archive)

Lt Gen Earle E. Partridge, a modest man yet a charismatic leader, commanded the 5th AF at the outbreak of war in Korea. (US National Archive)

completely unsuitable. Gen Almond established a GHQ Target Group on July 14 to allocate targets to FEAF aircraft, but with little input from qualified air staff, the targets were often inappropriate or in many cases (particularly bridge targets) they did not actually exist. Earlier, Gen Stratemeyer had requested that all aircraft operating over Korea should be under his operational control, so that their efforts could be properly coordinated, but this was refused by the US Navy. The US 7th Fleet was commanded by Vice-Admiral Arthur D. Struble, who did not wish to see his forces placed under Air Force command. Instead, backed by Admiral C. Turner Joy, Commander Naval Forces Far East, he requested – and was granted – exclusive use of a large airspace in the north of Korea, enabling the Navy to operate autonomously there. Attempts to coordinate the Naval Aviation and Air Force operations were further complicated by the Navy procedure of maintaining radio silence while at sea. Many of these problems were eventually resolved, but in the early part of the conflict they combined to frustrate operational planning and the proper use of air power.

In order to control future strategic bombing operations, Gen Stratemeyer placed all medium bomber units (including those that would deploy from the USA) under control of a new FEAF Bomber Command. This formation was established on July 8, 1950, under the command of Maj Gen Emmett O'Donnell. Having commanded bomber forces during World War II in Asia and Europe respectively, both O'Donnell and Partridge were advocates of strategic bombing. The new Bomber Command would exercise control over all B-29 units in the theatre: thus, FEAF would retain direct control of the strategic bomber force while 5th AF controlled all the land-based tactical aircraft operating over Korea. Stratemeyer envisaged that Bomber Command would interdict the lines of communication between the Han and Yalu Rivers, thereby cutting off the KPA from its strategic resupply and reinforcements; it would also destroy all industrial facilities that supported the North Korean war effort. Targeting policy was improved with the establishment by Gen MacArthur on July 22, 1950 – at the suggestion of Stratemeyer – of the Far East Command Target Selection Committee, staffed by airmen. In addition to the strategically important bridges over the Yalu and Han Rivers, the Target Selection Committee identified six main industrial centres that were to be attacked. These included Chinnampo (Nampo) and Pyongyang, both of which were in the west of the country and were centres respectively for metal production (including aluminium, copper and iron) and armaments industries. The other four cities were on the northeast coast: Hungnam was an important hub for light metals and chemicals, including explosives; Wonsan was the focus for oil refining and storage, as well as being a railway center; Chongjin boasted two harbours and an iron industry; and at Rashin (Rason) there was a major oil storage facility. However, political constraints soon proscribed Rashin because of its proximity to the Soviet border and the risk of inadvertent bombing of Soviet territory. Indeed, the whole of the bombing campaign was subject to stringent political limitations, in order not to alienate any of the UN allies whose support was crucial, and at the same time not to provoke Chinese or Soviet escalation of the conflict. For while the war in Korea was savage in the extreme, all the combatants were very careful to ensure that the conflict was limited to the Korean peninsula and could not spread any further.

The first strategic bombing campaign ran from July 13 until September 26, 1950, after which date the Joint Chiefs of Staff (JCS) declared that strategic attacks on the North Korean military infrastructure were no longer necessary. The UNC troops occupying much of the country now needed the bridges and power stations to remain intact. The feeling at the UNC headquarters was that the war was all but won and would end shortly. With victory apparently imminent, the 22nd and 92nd BGs were stood down and returned to the USA. However, the entry of the Chinese People's Volunteer Army on October 25 completely changed the strategic situation, and once again the UNC was caught unawares. While the initial reaction on November 4 was to start a series of fire-bombing raids against the North Korean towns of Kanggye, Sakchu, Pukchin and Sinuiju, a more measured directive issued the following day instructed the FEAF Bomber Command and Task Force 77 to start a two-week maximum effort against the southernmost spans and abutments of the Yalu bridges. The intention of this offensive was to stop the mass flow of troops and materiel across the border from Manchuria.

A further change of emphasis occurred with the introduction of the FEAF Interdiction Plan 4 in January 1951. Under this plan, the railway bridges, tunnels and marshalling yards would be attacked, with the intention of forcing the North Koreans and Chinese to use road transport instead. Since a single lorry could carry just 2 tons, as compared to the 20 tons carried by a railcar, a huge number of lorries would be needed to maintain the CPVA and KPA supply lines. At the time, such vehicles were believed to be in short supply. Furthermore, it was thought that road vehicles would be more vulnerable to attacks by tactical aircraft. Under the new plan, North Korea was divided into zones identified from 'A' to 'K' according to their priority: each zone would be targeted in sequence, with the air forces moving to the next zone once all the targets in the higher priority zone had been neutralized. Because of the threat to the B-29s by MiG-15s, the initial attacks in the highest priority Zone 'A,' in the vicinity of Sinuiju, were carried out by fighter-bombers. The naval aviators of TF 77

Maj Gen Emmett O'Donnell, a World War II bomber commander, was appointed as the first commander of FEAF Bomber Command. (NMUSAF)

were also asked to carry out a similar campaign in the northeast of the country, but Admiral Joy declined to do so, since at that time TF 77 aircraft were already fully committed to the close support of ground forces.

When it became clear in mid-February 1951 that fighter-bombers were not effective in the task, the strategic bomber force was directed to attack the targets in the northwest of the country. However, when the western arm of the North Korean rail system came under attack, the North Koreans simply switched to using the eastern arm. At this stage, Vice-Admiral Struble also agreed to TF 77 taking responsibility for Zones 'F' to 'H.' Successes by the B-29 force were achieved at considerable attrition, and by mid-April FEAF Bomber Command had only 75 aircraft available for operations against an agreed strength of 99 aircraft. The daily sortie rate was therefore halved from 24 missions to just 12 a day. In May 1951, Interdiction Plan 4 evolved into Operation *Strangle*, which had much the same objectives, although it was concentrated primarily against road transport in the area between the 39th Parallel (which ran roughly through Pyongyang and Wonsan) and CPVA/KPA rear areas.

The negotiations which opened at Kaesong on July 10, 1951, to establish an armistice in Korea, made little difference to the military campaign. Despite the talks, both sides continued their efforts to gain the most advantageous positions on the battlefield for themselves. Attacks on strategic targets continued through the summer, but on August 18, the FEAF, now under the command of Gen Otto P. Weyland, switched its attentions back to the North Korean railway system. Once again, B-29s were tasked to target bridges at Pyongyang, Sonchon, Sunchon and Sinanju, but the bridges at Huichon were deemed to be too far north; in attacking them, the Superfortresses would themselves be too vulnerable to MiG-15s.

From the start of the conflict, FEAF Bomber Command had sought to prevent the UAA from using airfields in Korea, and in October 1951, it turned its attention to neutralizing a series of newly constructed North Korean airfields. The airfields at Saamchaan, Taechon and Namsi were nearing completion and, mindful of the threat posed by MiG-15s flying from the Antung Complex, the first raid against them on October 13 was carried out at night. This attack caused some damage to the airfield, but it also served to demonstrate the limited accuracy of SHORAN-directed bombing. Subsequent attacks in mid-October were carried out in daylight and received the attention of the Antung-based MiG-15s. On 'Black Tuesday,' October 23, the Superfortress formations received a mauling from a large force of MiG-15s. As a result of this experience, the B-29 was withdrawn from daylight operations from October 28, and for the rest of the conflict the Superfortress crews operated primarily at night. Although some accuracy was sacrificed in the move to night operations, the bombers could once again venture into 'MiG Alley' to attack targets in the far northwest of North Korea. As the night campaign developed, so too did the need for ECM and for night-fighter sweep and escort.

In January 1952, FEAF target planners identified a chokepoint on the lateral rail line connecting the western and eastern coastlines. Near the village of Wadong, about 50 miles west of Wonsan, the rail line crossed an important east–west roadway at the bottom of a steep-sided gorge. In theory, it should have been possible to close down both the road and rail systems linking the two coasts by concentrated bombing in a small, easily defined area. For the next three months, B-26s and B-29s carried out an intensive bombing campaign against the Wadong Chokepoint, intending to cut both transport links. The lack of success with this approach led to a new strategic interdiction campaign, codenamed Operation *Saturate*, which also coordinated the efforts of the 5th AF and TF 77. *Saturate* started on March 3 and ran with some success until May, when UNC fighter-bomber aircraft losses made it impossible to sustain the campaign.

By the time that Operation *Saturate* had petered out, UNC commanders had already adopted a completely new strategy in the employment of air power over North Korea.

Gen Otto P. Weyland succeeded Stratemeyer as FEAF commander after the latter suffered a serious heart attack in 1951. (NMUSAF)

Rather than attempting to defeat the CPVA and KPA by interdicting their supply organization and thereby starving the front lines of food, ammunition and reinforcements, the new concept of 'Air Pressure' was designed to influence directly the North Korean delegation at the armistice negotiations, which were now taking place at Panmunjom. It was hoped that concentrated strikes on the infrastructure supporting various facets of everyday life in North Korea would force the delegates to progress the armistice more urgently. Large-scale coordinated attacks were planned against the electrical power generation and distribution system, as well as food production and industrial, transportation and strategic military targets. A change of senior commanders in 1952 had also brought a better working relationship between the UNC Air and Naval forces in Korea: Lt Gen Glenn O. Barcus, commander of the US 5th AF, and Vice-Admiral J. J. 'Jocko' Clark, commanding the US 7th Fleet, were good friends who worked well together, and this was reflected in closer operational ties between the services. The 'Air Pressure' concept also moved the emphasis of the strategic bombing role from attacks by B-29 medium bombers to mass strikes by F-84s and F-80 fighter-bombers and naval strike aircraft, supported by large-scale defence-suppression and fighter-escort missions.

Experienced fighter pilot Lt Gen Glenn O. Barcus took command of the US 5th AF in 1952. He worked closely with Vice Admiral Jocko Clark, who was also a personal friend. (NMUSAF)

The 'Air Pressure' campaign started with the raids against the hydroelectric power-generation system on June 23, 1952. Subsequent operations during the second half of the year included Operation *Pressure Pump*, large-scale airstrikes on 30 targets in Pyongyang on July 11, as well as another series of raids on Pyongyang on August 29. Although aircraft from TF 77 had participated in the power station and *Pressure Pump* raids, from October 1952 naval aircraft concentrated instead mainly on Battlefield Air Interdiction of CPVA/KPA tactical supply dumps. These missions were known as Cherokee Strikes, alluding to the native American ancestry of Vice-Admiral Clark.

In the next major phase of 'Air Pressure,' massed attacks were mounted against the reservoirs that provided water to the irrigation system for the rice-growing region immediately to the north of Pyongyang. The attacks were carried out from May 13–22, 1953, mainly by fighter-bomber units, although some B-29 missions were also tasked against these targets.

The thread that ran throughout the conflict was the campaign against airfields in North Korea. From the B-29 missions flown against Seoul airfield in the first days of the war until the last airstrikes by F-84s against Kanggye and Chunggangjin (Chunggang) in the last hours of the conflict, North Korean airfields were attacked periodically to deny their use to Soviet and UAA aircraft. Since the bases in China were off-limits to attack, the area of North Korea that was within range of the MiG-15 bases – in other words the area between the Yalu and Chongchon Rivers known as 'MiG Alley' – would always be contested, but keeping the North Korean airfields closed guaranteed UNC air superiority over the remainder of the country. It also meant that UAA ground-attack aircraft could never support their own ground forces. Whenever reconnaissance or intelligence indicated that damaged airfields were close to being completely repaired or that newly constructed airfields were nearly operational, missions were launched to destroy the runways. Missions also targeted aircraft deployed on the airfields whenever the KPAF attempted to establish forward operating bases. The armistice, which came into effect on July 27, 1953, was preceded by a frenzy of counter-air activity as UNC attempted to deny all the airfields in North Korea to the KPAF and to cause as much damage as possible to the North Korean military infrastructure.

Vice-Admiral J. J. 'Jocko' Clark, who had commanded a Battle Group during World War II, took command of the US 7th Fleet and TF 77 from 1952 and was an advocate of inter-service cooperation. (US National Archive)

THE CAMPAIGN
Industry, power and interdiction

Initial phase

B-29 Superfortress bombers of the 92nd BG dropping their bombload on a target in North Korea. B-29s dropped over 24 million pounds of ordnance during July and August 1950. (US National Archive)

On June 27, 1950, two days after the North Korean invasion, the 19th BG deployed from Guam to Kadena Air Base on the Japanese island of Okinawa in order to be in striking distance of targets in Korea. The first missions were flown the following day: in the late afternoon of June 28, four aircraft set out for an armed reconnaissance sortie over the area to the north and east of Seoul. The bombers split into two pairs: one pair followed the railway northwards from Seoul to Kapyong while the other pair followed the line eastwards towards Uijongbu, attacking targets of opportunity on the roads and railways. These were tactical armed reconnaissance sorties rather than the strategic strikes for which the crews were trained, and they illustrate the ambiguity between strategic and tactical interdiction which continued through the whole conflict.

The B-29s of the 19th BG were in action again over the next two days. The following morning, bombing from just 3,000ft, nine Superfortresses targeted the buildings at Kimpo airfield (K-14), which was now in KPAF hands. Meanwhile, two more aircraft bombed the railway station in Seoul. Two KPAF Yak-9Ps scrambled from their new forward base at Kimpo to intercept the bombers, but the B-29 gunners claimed to have shot down one Yak and damaged the other. On July 30, a formation of B-29s from the 19th BG was escorted by F-51 Mustangs of 77 Squadron RAAF to bomb the airfield at Yonpo (K-27). Reconnaissance photographs of Yonpo taken two days earlier had shown over 60 KPAF Il-10s at the airfield, but by the time of the B-29 attack, most of those aircraft had already redeployed to Wonsan (K-25), Kimpo, and the forward operating strip at Pyonggang (K-21), leaving only 15 aircraft at Yonpo. The B-29s delivered all of their bombs accurately within the airfield perimeter, but the KPAF aircraft parked there remained unscathed.

As the KPA advanced, the bridges over the Han River, to the immediate south of Seoul, became the arteries through which it was resupplied and reinforced. Realizing the vital importance of the bridges, Gen Stratemeyer directed FEAF bombers to target them, and the first attack was carried out by 19th BG on July 1. Crews were ordered to bomb individually and to drop single bombs until their target had been destroyed. However, the bridges proved to be difficult targets to hit, and it would not be until mid-August that the last bridge was brought down. Most of the missions flown by the 19th BG over the next days were in tactical support of UNC forces.

FEAF Bomber Command was formally established on July 8, 1950, by which time reinforcements, in the shape of two more B-29-equipped BGs, had begun to arrive in theatre. The 22nd BG deployed from its base at March AFB, California, to Kadena on July 8, while the 92nd BG from Spokane, Washington, deployed to Yokota, just to the west of Tokyo. Unlike the 19th BG, the aircraft from mainland USA were equipped with the AN/APG-13 radar which gave them a capability to bomb targets 'blind' through cloud, whereas the 19th BG aircraft were limited to visual attacks. The arrival of aircraft with an all-weather capability was a major benefit to the FEAF bomber force in the midst of the summer monsoon. The new arrivals mounted their first operational mission on July 13, when 50 B-29s from the 22nd and 92nd BGs carried out a radar-aimed bombing raid through the clouds against the oil refinery and railway marshalling yards at Wonsan.

Naval aircraft from Carrier Air Group 5 (CVG-5) operating from the aircraft carrier USS *Valley Forge* (CV-45), had been involved in tactical airstrikes from the west coast during the first week of July, and after replenishing at Okinawa, *Valley Forge* arrived in Korean waters once again on July 18. This time it was stationed in the Sea of Japan to support that day's amphibious landing of the US 1st Cavalry Division at Pohang. That evening, Skyraiders and Corsairs attacked the oil refinery at Wonsan, finding it apparently undamaged by the B-29 attack five days previously. The naval aircraft left the facility wrecked and aflame. At dawn the following morning, CVG-5 launched 13 Skyraiders,

Two important railway bridges near Pakchon, 40 miles north of Pyongyang, under attack by B-29s led by Capt Leslie J. Westberg (a World War II veteran who was later promoted to brigadier general) on July 27, 1950. (US National Archive)

19 Corsairs, and 24 Grumman F9F Panthers against targets in North Korea. The primary target for the Skyraiders and Corsairs was the Bogun (Motomiya) chemical plant at Hamhung, while the Panthers attacked the airfields at Hamhung West (K-28), Sondok (K-26) and Yonpo (K-27).

For the remainder of July, the FEAF bombers were involved in tactical tasks, although they continued to attack bridges and to pressure the KPAF bases: the airfields at Pyongyang Heijo (K-23) and Pyongyang East (K-24) were bombed on July 20 by 14 B-29s. The losses inflicted upon the KPAF during the airfield attacks on July 18 and 19, as well as those incurred during air-to-air combat in the previous few days, left it with only a handful of aircraft and pilots. Nevertheless, KPAF aircraft continued the fight: on July 19, three Yak-9Ps severely damaged a B-29 of the 19th BG over the west railway bridge at Seoul.

Industrial targets

FEAF was finally authorized by the JCS, via Gen MacArthur, on July 31 to commence a strategic bombing campaign against the North Korean industrial base. The intention was to cut off at their source all supplies of arms, armaments and military equipment by destroying factories and the rail distribution network. However, the bombers were prohibited from using mass incendiary weapons in case fire-bombing might be exploited for propaganda by the North Koreans. Two further BGs would also be transferred to FEAF to help with the new task. In fact, FEAF planners had already pre-empted the order and the first raid on the industrial sites clustered around Hungnam had taken place the previous day. As the poor summer weather had precluded a visual attack, RB-29 Superfortresses of the 31st Strategic Reconnaissance Squadron (SRS) had been tasked to photograph the radar scope view of the target area before detailed mission planning began. With good contrast between the radar returns from sea and land, the location of Hungnam on a distinctive headland on the eastern coastline made it an ideal radar target. The Chosen Nitrogen Explosives factory, which had the most conspicuous radar return, was selected as the first target; it was bombed by a force of 47 B-29s from the 22nd and 92nd BGs, which attacked through solid cloud on the morning of July 30. Two days later, 46 B-29s mounted a follow-up raid against the Chosen Nitrogen Fertilizer factory in the same area. This time the weather was clear and the bombers were able to aim their weapons visually. After another day-long break, 39 bombers returned to Hungnam on August 3 to bomb the Bogun chemical plant, dropping through cloud from 16,000ft.

Although the strategic campaign had started, interdiction tasking was still a priority and the railway marshalling yards at Seoul were bombed by B-29s on August 4 and 5. Meanwhile, the two extra BGs promised to FEAF had arrived in theatre: the 98th BG from Spokane deployed to Yokota and the 307th BG, based at MacDill AFB in Florida, deployed to Kadena. This reinforcement brought the number of B-29s in theatre to around 130. From then onwards, three B-29 Bomber Groups concentrated on industrial targets in North Korea, while the other two attacked interdiction targets, in particular the road and railway bridges. In this way, major attacks on North Korean industrial facilities were mounted every three or four days, interspersed with interdiction missions on the other days.

By now, the KPAF fighter force was no longer effective, and nor were there many large-calibre AAA guns in North Korea, so the bombers enjoyed the security of air supremacy over the Korean peninsula. The main challenge to the bombers was the weather, either because of storm clouds or strong jet streams. For this reason, an airborne mission commander flew in a weather reconnaissance aircraft ahead of the main force. He had the authority to decide if the target could be attacked by radar or if the bombing force should divert to an alternate target. Bombing runs were planned along the best axis for radar attacks, ideally by sections

The Wonsan oil refinery is left burning after the attack on July 18, 1950, by aircraft of CVG-5 operating from USS *Valley Forge* (CV-45) The smoke from these fires was visible from the carrier, operating at sea off the Korean east coast. (US National Archive)

of three bombers flying in 'vee' formation and releasing their weapons when the lead aircraft dropped its bombload. However, if the weather at bombing altitude was unsuitable for formation flying, the mission commander could order a 'Hometown' attack in which the aircraft would drop into one-minute trail and aim their bombs individually using their radar.

The next major raid by B-29s was against the naval oil storage facility at Rashin. The US State Department had expressed concerns about Rashin as a target because of its location just 17 miles from the Soviet border. The fear was that if any bombs fell astray, they would land in the USSR. The JCS had therefore directed that any bombs dropped on Rashin must be visually aimed. Unfortunately, that decision had not been communicated to FEAF, meaning the attack on August 12 was radar-aimed and rather inaccurate: all the bombs fell in the countryside outside the city, although Soviet soil was not touched. A second attempt to bomb Rashin using visual aiming ten days later was defeated by the weather, the bombers attacking Chongjin instead. However, this was enough for Rashin to be deleted from the target list, for the time being at least.

Meanwhile, the FEAF bombers had continued their efforts to destroy all of the bridges over the Han River. The task had been given to the 19th BG as it was the only unit with the requisite bomb shackles for carrying 2,000lb bombs, which were thought to be the best weapon for the job. Despite the repeated efforts of the B-29 crews since late July, one bridge – the West Bridge, a robust steel structure which carried the railway over the river – steadfastly refused to fall. Because of its seeming invulnerability to bombs, it became known as the 'elastic bridge'. Frustrated at the inability of FEAF to hit the bridge, Gen Stratemeyer promised a crate of whisky to the unit which destroyed it. On the morning of August 19, the bridge was bombed by the 19th BG and the crews were

The wreckage of a locomotive in the bombed-out northwest marshalling yards at Pyongyang, after bombing raids by FEAF B-29s. (US National Archive)

confident that they had at least damaged it. Later in the day, it was attacked again by Corsairs and Skyraiders of CVG-11 operating from USS *Philippine Sea* (CV-47), which had recently joined TF 77 and was sailing off the west coast of Korea. While the B-29s attacked from altitudes that kept them immune from the small-calibre AAA guns near the target, the naval aircraft had to approach at much lower altitudes and were vulnerable to gunfire. As he led the carrier air group into the attack, the commanding officer, Cdr R. W. Vogel, was shot down and killed by AAA fire. Nevertheless, his pilots carried out a successful attack and claimed a number of hits on the bridge structure; but when they left the target area, the bridge still seemed to be intact. The next morning, a formation of B-29s returned for another attempt, but when they arrived overhead, they saw that two spans of the bridge had collapsed overnight. They soon finished the job by dropping a third span. Good to his word, Stratemeyer dispatched the promised crates of whisky to both the 19th BG and CVG-11.

In the last week of August, FEAF bombers carried out four more major attacks on North Korean industrial sites: on August 25, Hungnam was revisited, while Songjin was bombed on August 28 and Chongjin on the 30th. On the last day of the month, B-29s bombed the metal works at Chinnampo. Meanwhile, the B-29 force also continued the campaign to destroy all the bridges in North Korea. Given the difficulty in attacking these relatively small yet immensely strong targets, FEAF experimented with radio-guided bombs. In August 1950, a Special Projects Section was formed within the 19th BG in order to trial the use of the VB-3 RAZON 1,000lb guided bomb in combat. Led by Lt Col Walter G. Cannon, the section comprised selected maintenance crews and 14 operational B-29 crews. The weapon comprised a standard AN-M65 bomb fitted with a tail unit incorporating flying controls and a radio receiver, a gyro unit to provide stabilization, and a one-million-candle power flare for sighting. It was aimed using a Norden bombsight modified with the 'Crab' and 'Jag' attachments. 'Crab' enabled the image of the sighting flare to be superimposed into the aiming telescope so that the bombardier could track it in relation to the target, while controlling the weapon via the radio link; 'Jag' altered the bombsight rate of change to allow for the different ballistics and time of flight of the guided weapon in comparison to an unguided bomb.

Maintenance crews experienced a steep learning curve as they gained familiarity with the weapon. Many of the bombs had been damaged in storage, and these issues were further complicated by problems with bomb loading and with weapon electrical connections. A Superfortress could carry six RAZON bombs. Trials in the USA had already established that the best accuracy with the weapon was achieved from 15,000ft, but that it could be dropped from as high as 21,000ft. Although radio-guided weapons promised excellent accuracy against bridge targets, they could only be used in limited tactical situations. Firstly, they were restricted to good weather and daylight as the bombardier had to stay in visual contact with both target and weapon throughout the attack. Secondly, for the same reason and since the field of view of the bombsight was quite narrow, the bomber could not perform any evasive manoeuvring during the attack, so the weapon could only be employed against lightly defended targets. Consequently, the opportunities to use RAZON operationally over Korea were very limited.

The lead B-29 of 19th BG unloads its bombs onto a target in North Korea on the 150th combat mission flown by the formation since the start of the war. (US National Archive)

B-29s of the 98th BG over North Korea in September 1950, as the first phase of the strategic bombing campaign drew to a close. (US National Archive)

The first RAZON mission was carried out on August 23, 1950, but most of the missions carried out between then and September 28 were unsuccessful because of both technical and operational teething problems. However, after a brief break while the bombs were reworked and tactics were consolidated, the accuracy increased dramatically. A total of 389 RAZON bombs were dropped operationally in Korea; however, only 15 bridges were destroyed in these attacks, because operational missions were also used as opportunities for training. If, for example, a bombardier destroyed two bridges with two bombs, he was encouraged to drop the remaining four bombs on targets that had already been destroyed for the practice.

The amphibious landings carried out well behind the North Korean lines at Inchon near Seoul on September 15 marked a turning point in the war and a change of emphasis for both the strategic bombing campaign and the bridge interdiction missions. The remaining bridges would now be needed by UNC forces as they broke out of the Inchon beachhead and the Pusan perimeter, and advanced into North Korea. The industrial infrastructure would also be needed to rebuild North Korea while it was occupied by UNC forces. By this stage of the war, FEAF was in any case already running out of strategic targets. The last mission of this first phase of the strategic bombing campaign was flown on September 26 by the 92nd BG against the Fusen (Pujon) hydroelectric power-generating plant, about 40 miles north of Hungnam.

Strategic interdiction

Having run out of strategic industrial targets in mid-September, FEAF B-29s concentrated instead on attacking known KPA training camps. The intention was to weaken the KPA by causing casualties amongst its recruits and undermining their morale, as well as destroying the military training facilities. On September 20, FEAF bombers struck the three barracks which comprised the North Korean Military Academy, and three days later they bombed a troop training center in Hamhung. A training center at Nanam, near Chogjin on the

northeast coast, was targeted on October 2, followed ten days later by another military training center at Hungnam.

In another directive from FEAF, a target list of 33 bridges was passed to Bomber Command in October. By October 20, 108 RAZON bombs had been dropped on bridges, destroying spans on six of them. However, such was the paucity of targets that the FEAF bomber force reduced its sortie rate to just 25 a day, and two B-29 units – the 22nd and 92nd BGs – were stood down to return to the USA on October 22. It was on that day that UNC forces crossed the Chongchon River, buoyed with a sense of impending victory. No-one in the UNC command chain foresaw that China would intervene directly in the conflict.

The war entered its next phase when the CPVA launched its first attack on UNC forces on October 25, driving UNC troops back over the Chongchon River in a few days. The strategic bombing response was to start an incendiary campaign against the northernmost cities of North Korea. These cities were thought to be both arsenals and shelters for the CPVA/KPA, and the aim of this campaign was to neutralize the troops and military equipment sheltered there. The new bombing offensive started on November 4 with an incendiary raid directed against Kanggye, but the B-29 crews of the 98th BG found their target covered by cloud and dropped their bombs on Chongjin instead. Kanggye was attacked in fine weather the next day by 21 B-29s of the 19th BG. By this time yet another dimension had been added to the conflict: the entry of the MiG-15 into combat. In response to the UNC advance into North Korea, the 151st GvIAD (comprising the 28th and 72nd GvIAPs) had deployed to Mukden and Anshan, and the 28th IAD (67th IAP and 139th GvIAP) had moved to Liaoyang in

Just above the centre of the photo, a USN AD-3 Skyraider pulls out from a dive-bombing pass after releasing a 2,000lb bomb during a raid on the bridges across the Yalu River at Sinuiju in mid-November 1950. Note the numerous bomb craters near the bridges. (US National Archive)

The bridges over the Yalu River at Sinuiju, under attack by aircraft from USS *Leyte* (CV-32) on November 14, 1950. Three spans of the road bridge have been dropped but the railway bridge (the lower bridge) appears to be intact. (US National Archive)

order to secure Chinese airspace. However, their remit was enlarged to cover the industrial area to the south of the Yalu River, around Sinuiju. The first MiG-15 combat missions – defensive patrols over the Sinuiju bridges – were flown on November 1.

Bombing the bridges

Gen MacArthur directed on November 5 that the Korean ends of all the bridges which connected Korea to Manchuria were also to be destroyed. Of particular interest were the Sinuiju bridges, two substantial structures – one carrying the road and the other carrying the railway – which connected Sinuiju to Antung. MacArthur was overruled the next day by President Truman, who wanted to prohibit attacks against targets within 5 miles of the Yalu River, but later in the same day the President was persuaded by the argument that the bridges were the key structures supporting the CPVA advance. However, the authorization to bomb the bridges was qualified by the restriction that crews were not to cross into China. This constrained the possible attack directions, causing a particular problem for B-29 crews attempting to bomb the solidly built ¾-mile-long bridges at Sinuiju. Crews would also have to bomb from above 18,000ft in order to remain clear of the heavy-calibre AAA fire, making weapon aiming against such narrow targets a very difficult challenge that was further exacerbated by strong crosswinds at altitude.

A raid by B-29s against the two bridges at Sinuiju was planned for November 7 but was delayed for 24 hours because of the weather. The following day, a force of 79 bombers set out for the bridges. Before they arrived over the target, flights of F-51s and F-80s had been tasked with suppressing AAA in the area. Eight MiG-15s of the 72nd GvIAP launched to intervene, and during the ensuing mêlée at 18,000ft, 1st Lt R. J. Brown, flying an F-80 from the 16th FIS, scored hits on the MiG-15 of Sen Lt A. E. Sanin. The latter aircraft disengaged by diving steeply and jettisoning its external fuel tanks, leading Brown to believe that he had shot down the MiG; however, Sanin landed safely, though damaged, at Mukden. None of the B-29s were damaged during the raid, but the target bridges also remained untouched.

The next day, November 9, dawned cold but clear, with excellent visibility, and another 'maximum effort' naval airstrike was launched against the Sinuiju railway bridge by USS *Philippine Sea* and *Valley Forge*. Eight MiG-15s from the 28th GvIAP and another six from the 72nd GvIAP were launched to intercept these raids. The Soviet pilots were successfully held off by the Panther escorts, and the Skyraiders and Corsairs were able to carry out their attacks unmolested by enemy aircraft, although they were unable to hit the bridge. Later that morning, an RB-29 of the 31st SRS which was attempting to photograph the area of Sinuiju was intercepted by MiG-15s from the 72nd GvIAP. Diving through the F-80 fighter escorts, MiG-15 pilots Maj A. Z. Bordun and Sen Lt L. M. Dymchenko engaged the Superfortress, damaging it severely and shooting out two engines. The aircraft staggered back to Japan but crashed short of the runway at Johnson Air Base on the outskirts of Tokyo. This combat loss marked a turning point in the strategic air campaign, for air supremacy over Korea had been lost.

Naval airstrikes and FEAF bomber raids against the bridges over the Yalu continued over the next five days. Flying from USS *Leyte* (CV-32) on November 10, aircraft from CVG-3 mounted 83 sorties against the Sinuiju railway bridge. Once again, the Panther escorts were able to keep the MiG-15s away from the Corsair and Skyraider strike aircraft. Fighter escorts, this time F-80s, also foiled an attack by the MiG-15s of the 72nd GvIAP which attempted to engage two B-29s near Sinuiju. However, about an hour later, B-29s from the 307th BW

This B-29 of the 19th BG ('Snugglebunny') was badly damaged during a bombing raid on the bridges over the Yalu River on March 1, 1951, and was forced to divert to Seoul (K-16). It eventually completed 45 missions over North Korea. (US National Archive)

OPPOSITE BRIDGES 1953

From 10 to 20 January, 1953, the UNC air forces conducted a major bombing campaign against the bridges systems over the Taeryong and Chongchon Rivers, as well as the large switching and marshalling yard at Maengjungni which lay between the two rivers. Earlier in the conflict, the North Koreans had constructed a fan of bypass crossings over each river to maintain the traffic flow.

A MiG-15 of the 176th GvIAP (324th IAD), flown by Senior Lieutenant A. P. Gogolev (two victories in Korea), at Antung in April 1951. The arrival of the MiG-15 over North Korea marked the end of UNC air supremacy in 'MiG Alley.' (Krylov & Tepsurkaev)

which were bombing the town of Uiju, some 10 miles upstream of Sinuiju, were less lucky. Eight more MiG-15s from the 139th GvIAP, led by Maj G. I. Kharkovsky, intercepted them, and despite the efforts of the UNC fighter escorts, Kharkovsky and his wingman, Lt Yu. I. Akimov, shot down one bomber and damaged another.

As well as having to run the gauntlet of Soviet fighters, UNC bombers operating near the Yalu River also had to contend with increasingly heavy antiaircraft fire. After several months without casualties from ground artillery, a B-29 was badly damaged by AAA guns on November 12 while bombing the bridge across the Yalu River at Manpojin (Manpo), some 120 miles northeast of Sinuiju.

Raids against the Sinuiju bridges continued on November 12, 14 and 18, but the only success against the bridges was achieved by a combined strike by USS *Leyte* and *Valley Forge* on November 12, which dropped one span of the Sinuiju road bridge. During these missions, the fighter escorts proved quite successful in keeping the MiG-15s away from the B-29s, although two Superfortresses were seriously damaged by MiG-15s on November 14. B-29s also continued the incendiary campaign, burning many of the towns and cities in North Korea that were thought to be sheltering KPA and CPVA troops, supplies or equipment. During the next week, the weather turned, heavy clouds bringing snow and freezing conditions. Operations were also hampered by the lack of daylight, for by now there were less than 11 hours of daylight each day.

By November 19, the Yalu River was sufficiently frozen to carry road traffic, making the bridges over the river less critical for the KPA/CPVA supply lines. Nevertheless, FEAF renewed

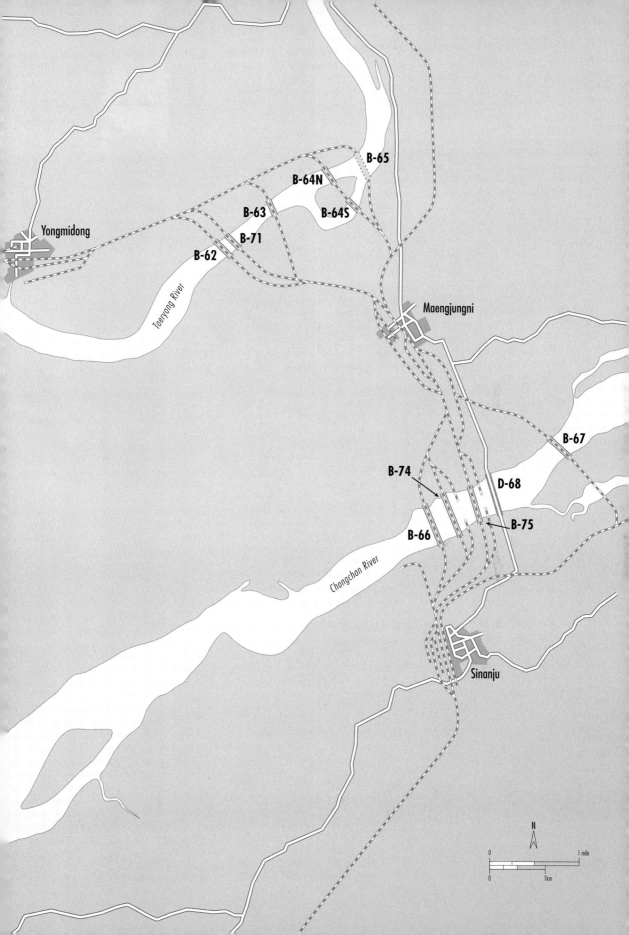

Yongmidong

Taeryong River

B-65

B-64N

B-63

B-64S

B-71

B-62

Maengjungni

B-67

B-74

D-68

B-66

B-75

Chongchon River

Sinanju

N

0   1 mile

0   1km

A 12,000lb TARZON radio-guided bomb loaded into a B-29. After initial teething troubles, the weapon enjoyed some success, particularly against the bridge at Kanggye on January 13, 1951. (US National Archive)

its attacks on the bridges over the Yalu in support of the UNC ground offensive which started on November 24. The B-29 raids succeeded in dropping one span of the railway bridge at Manpojin on November 25 and two spans of the road bridge at Chongsonjin (Chongson) the next day. However, these successes made little difference to the strategic situation, since that night saw the start of a Chinese counteroffensive which threw UNC ground forces onto the defensive. Over the course of the next three months, massed attacks by the CPVA forced UNC troops steadily southwards and back across the Han River.

RAZON attacks continued until December 1950, when they were temporarily suspended in favour of the 12,000lb VB-13 TARZON, which was thought would be more effective against bridges. The much larger TARZON weapons were too big to fit into the B-29 bomb bay, so three aircraft were modified to carry just one weapon each, semi-recessed below the fuselage. In addition, the nose glass in the bombardier position in these aircraft was replaced by B-50 nose glass to remove internal reflections that had been causing problems with aiming the RAZONs.

Just as they had with RAZON, the 19th BG Special Project Section experienced teething problems with TARZON. Somewhat embarrassingly, the first mission failed when the weapon could not be released from the aircraft. The fault was later traced to work that had been carried out on the photographic circuits, during which the power to the S-4 bomb shackle had been erroneously disconnected. Once again, a reworking of the weapons and amendments to the procedures for uncaging the gyros and tuning the radio guidance receivers solved many of the problems, producing a dramatic increase in the success rate. On January 13, 1951, faith in the weapon was vindicated when two spans of the railway bridge at Kanggye were dropped by a single TARZON.

In response to the appearance of MiG-15s over Korea, the USAF had transferred the Republic F-84E Thunderjets of the 27th FEG from Bergstrom AFB, Texas, and the

North American F-86A Sabres of the 4th FIG from Wilmington, Delaware, to FEAF. Both units flew their first operational missions over Korea in December, but it was soon apparent that while the F-86 was a good match for the MiG-15, the F-84 was more suited to ground-attack missions than the fighter-escort role. The 4th FIG was based at Johnson AFB near Tokyo, and although some aircraft flew from forward operating bases in Korea, they did not have the range to escort bombers as far as the Yalu River. For this reason, B-29s were not tasked into Interdiction Area 'A' close to the Yalu when FEAF opened its Interdiction Plan 4 in mid-December. Instead, the responsibility for covering targets in the area was passed to the fighter-bomber groups. Indeed, there was little strategic bombing activity in December and January, although 63 B-29s bombed Pyongyang with incendiary bombs on January 3, 1951, and another 60 B-29s attacked the city again two days later.

On the morning of January 21, two flights of F-84s from the 27th FEG dive-bombed a bridge over the Chongchon near Anju when they were bounced by six MiG-15s from the 29th GvIAP, accompanied by Chinese pilots from the 10th Flight Regiment. During this engagement, Li Han scored the first kill for the PLAAF when he shot down the F-84 flown by Lt G. W. Simpson. Two days later, the 5th Air Force mounted two major airstrikes to neutralize the KPAF operations from Sinuiju (K-30) and Pyongyang (K-23) airfields. In the first, 33 F-84s from the 27th FEG carried out a dawn attack on Sinuiju airfield. The Soviet and Chinese airmen were taken by surprise and two flights of F-84s had completed their strafing runs by the time the first MiG-15s took off from Antung. In the ensuing mêlée between the F-84s and 20 Soviet MiG-15s, supported by another eight Chinese MiG-15s, two Soviet MiGs were severely damaged and another was shot down, while two Chinese MiG-15s were also lost. The Soviet pilots claimed six kills against F-84s, but no losses were recorded by the USAF that day, although it seems likely that a number of aircraft were badly damaged. During the combat, Lt J. Kratt of the 523rd FES was credited with two MiG-15 kills.

Armament crews load a pair of 1,000lb Mk 65 bombs onto an F-84 of the 49th FBG at Taegu. (US National Archive)

Later in the morning, a force of 46 F-80s from 49th FBG strafed the AAA batteries around Pyongyang before 21 B-29s of the 19th and 309th BGs from Okinawa bombed the airfield. However, the focus of Interdiction Plan 4 for the FEAF bomber force was on the bridges on the east coast railway line. On February 1, B-29s of the 307th BG destroyed nine bridge spans along the line between Kyongsong and Hamhung. An intensive three-day effort starting on February 7 took down more bridges, but the weather was turning and on February 9 the B-29s bombed Hamhung by radar.

A rearming and refueling detachment for F-86s had been established at Suwon on February 22; however, even these arrangements could not generate enough F-86s to provide fighter-escort cover to B-29s operating in 'MiG Alley.' On the other hand, F-80s operating from Suwon and Taegu did have sufficient numbers and range to do so, but it would be on the limits of their tactical range and they would only be able to spend a few minutes in the target area. Using this compromise arrangement, some small-scale B-29 formations escorted by F-80s raided into the north during February 1951. On February 25, a box of four B-29s bombed the rail and road bridges at Kaechon, 10 miles east of Anju, but were intercepted by 12 MiG-15s from the 28th GvIAP. The MiG pilots carried out a sustained attack against the bombers, which maintained tight formation and kept up heavy defensive fire. Having seen their shells registering on the B-29s and smoke issuing from some of the aircraft, the Soviet pilots had to disengage as they ran short of fuel. They confidently reported that they had damaged at least three bombers, but they were credited by their command center with having shot down all four aircraft. In fact, no losses were reported by FEAF.

By late February, it was clear that the fighter-bombers were not effective at long-range bombing operations against the Yalu bridges. As a result, FEAF bombers began to be tasked into Interdiction Area 'A' from March 1. On that day, 18 B-29s from the 98th BG were tasked against the bridge at Kogunyong (Cheonggang) between Chongju (Jeongju) and Sinuiju. After taking off from Yokota, the bombers were delayed by un-forecast winds, so they arrived late at the rendezvous point with their escort of 22 F-80s. In consequence, the F-80s ran short of fuel and had to turn back early, leaving the B-29s to continue unescorted to their target. Inevitably, they were intercepted by two flights of MiG-15s from the 28th

'Carlson's Canyon', the railway bridge and tunnel complex south of Kilchu, that became a battle of wits between naval aviators and North Korean engineers in March and April 1951. This image is dated March 2, 1951, before much damage had been done, and the supports for the unfinished parallel bridge are visible on the near side of the rail bridge. (US National Archive)

GvIAP, led by Maj P. B. Ovsyannikov and Lt Col V. I. Kolyadin. The MiG-15s caught the B-29s just as they turned for home and subjected them to a heavy attack, leaving ten of the Superfortresses severely damaged. Three of the bombers were hit so badly that they had to make emergency landings at Taegu. It was this mission that brought home the fact that UNC had now lost air superiority over northwest Korea. Once again, the B-29s were temporarily withdrawn from operations in 'MiG Alley' between the Yalu and Chongchon Rivers.

Bridges continued to make up most of the targets allocated to the FEAF strategic bomber force. In early March, the 98th and 307th BGs were issued with suitable bomb racks to enable them to carry the 2,000lb bombs which had already proven the best weapons to use against bridges. The 19th BG also continued with its trials of the TARZON bombs and achieved six successful attacks during early March. By the third week in March, the 4th FIG was confident that its F-86s could now support B-29 missions into 'MiG Alley' and the Superfortresses began to receive tasks against bridges in the far north of Korea. On March 23, three formations of B-29s from the 19th and 307th BGs were escorted northwards by F-86s. The bombers attacked the bridges at Kogunyong, Kwaksan and Chonjun, as well as several more bridges on the railway line between Sinuiju and Sinanju. The Superfortresses were in action again the following day against bridges on the Manpojin–Sinanju line.

Meanwhile, the strategic importance of the Sinuiju bridges had increased in late March as the Yalu River began to thaw. The ice could no longer support vehicles or pedestrians, and the remaining bridges again became the only means of crossing the river. On March 29, B-29s from the 19th and 307th BGs were sent on missions against the bridge at Manpojin, while three TARZON-loaded B-29s from the 19th BG headed for the important Sinuiju bridges. The main force encountered poor weather in their target area, so instead they bombed their alternate target at Pyongyang airfield. However, the TARZON formation pressed ahead, but the mission was plagued with bad luck from the start. One aircraft was forced to abort the mission and return to base with a broken engine oil pipe, and the other two aircraft came under attack from 18 MiG-15s in the target area. These Soviet fighters were from the 28th and 72nd GvIAP, led by Lt Col N. L. Trofimov. During the engagement, the MiG-15s inflicted enough damage on the B-29 (45-21749) flown by the Group commander, Lt Col Payne Jennings, that two engines were shut down and the aircraft had to abort the mission; it subsequently crashed into the sea as it attempted to return to base, killing the entire crew. The remaining B-29 did release its TARZON, but the weapon missed its target and the aircraft was itself so badly damaged by the MiG-15s that it had to divert to an alternative airfield. Here it

TARZON attack on Sinuiju bridges on 29 March, 1951

A head-on view of a B-29 Superfortress (serial number 45-21745) of the 19th Bombardment Group at 15,000ft on a clear day over North Korea. The bomber has just released a 12,000lb TARZON radio-guided bomb, aimed at the bridge across the Yalu River at Sinuiju and is itself under attack from a Soviet MiG-15 fighter. On 29 March 1951, B-29 Superfortresses from the 19th and 307th BGs were tasked against the bridges over the Yalu River at Manpojin and Sinanju. While the main force headed for Manpojin, three TARZON-loaded B-29s from the 19th BG headed for the important Sinuiju bridges. The main force encountered poor weather in their target area and instead they bombed their alternate target at Pyongyang airfield. However, the TARZON formation pressed ahead, but one aircraft was forced to abort the mission and return to base with a broken engine oil pipe. Then, in the target area, the remaining two aircraft came under attack from 18 MiG-15s. These Soviet fighters were from 28th and 72nd GvIAP led by Lt Col N.L. Trofimov. During the engagement, the MiG-15s inflicted enough damage on the B-29 (45-21749) flown by the Group commander, Lt Col Payne Jennings, that two engines were shut down and the aircraft had to abort the mission; it subsequently crashed into the sea as it attempted to return to base, killing the entire crew. The remaining B-29, pictured here, released its TARZON but the weapon missed its target and the aircraft was itself so badly damaged by the MiG-15s that it had to divert to an alternative airfield.

B-29s of the 98th BG attacking a target in North Korea. FEAF Bomber Command responded to the Chinese offensive in October 1950 with incendiary attacks on towns that were thought to be sheltering enemy troops. (US National Archive)

was discovered that the battle damage was so extensive that the aircraft could not return to its base for five days.

Despite this setback, missions against the other bridges over the Yalu continued over the next two days. On March 30, B-29s from the 19th, 98th and 307th BGs successfully dropped a span of the rail bridge at Manpojin and two spans of the road bridge at Chingsongjin (Cheongsu), some 35 miles upstream of Sinuiju. They also bombed a pontoon bridge at Chongsongjin. A raid the following day against the road bridge at Linchiang, in the far north of Korea, was less successful, perhaps because it was carried out by new replacement crews who had only recently arrived in the Far East. Cloud cover prevented bombing attacks against the Yalu bridges during the first days of April. Linchiang was due to be attacked again on April 7 by 19th BG, but fog over the target meant that the bombers dropped their weapons on an alternate target on the east coast. On the same day, 16 B-29s set out for the bridges at Uiju and Sinuiju: aircraft from the 307th BG hit the bridge at Uiju, while those of the 98th BG bombed that at Sinuiju. Despite accurate bombing which straddled the bridge during this latter attack, its structure was apparently untouched.

Five days later, FEAF made a final attempt to destroy the bridge at Sinuiju. This time the bomber force was to consist of 48 B-29s drawn from all three BGs. A single TARZON bomber was included amongst the Superfortresses, the remainder of which were armed with 2,000lb bombs. The B-29s were to be escorted by 54 F-84s from the 27th FEG, with high cover provided by F-86s of the 4th FIG. Unfortunately, a number of bombers experienced technical issues, so by the time the bomber formation set out for the target, there were only 39 B-29s and the formation had become stretched out. As they approached Sinuiju, the first formation – comprising eight B-29s from the 19th BG – was intercepted by four sections of MiG-15s, each of six or eight fighters, from the 196th IAP and 176th GvIAP which had taken off from Antung. Despite the efforts of the escort fighters, the 28 MiG-15s were able to get through to the bombers, carrying out high-speed firing passes on their quarry. In the chaos of close combat, the F-84 pilots became confused and started shooting at F-86s as well as MiG-15s. The lead bomber, 'Dragon Lady' (44-61835) of the 19th BG, was hit on the left-hand side of the cockpit, killing the pilot, 1st Lt Gene E. Wright, and the bombardier; despite being wounded, the co-pilot, 1st Lt Willis E. Umholtz, continued the bombing run and then successfully diverted the aircraft to Suwon. 'Hot Box' (44-69682) and 'Lucky Dog' (44-86370) from the same group were less fortunate: the former was shot down over the target area and the latter crashed into the sea while trying to return to base with an engine on fire. A third bomber from the 19th BG, 'No Sweat' (44-87618), diverted to Seoul with heavy damage and having lost two engines. During the attack by the 19th BG formation, the TARZON round missed its target.

A further four MiG-15s from the 176th GvIAD, which joined the fray 15 minutes later, became entangled with the escort fighters, but eight more MiG-15s from the 196th IAP, led by Kpt B. V. Bokach, intercepted the second bomber formation, comprising 12 B-29s from the 307th BG. Two bombers were lost from this formation: 'Wolf Pack' (44-86343) was shot down over the target and another Superfortress, flown by Capt James M. Chenault, which was being used for ECM support, was severely damaged when it dropped out of formation because of engine trouble. The rear crew abandoned the bomber, but Chenault managed to reach Suwon, where the remainder of the crew parachuted to safety. Kpt B. S. Abakumov was credited with shooting down one of these bombers, but his aircraft was badly damaged afterwards by an F-86. The rear gunner of a 19th BG Superfortress, Sgt Lyle R. Patterson, also claimed the destruction of a MiG-15, although it is likely that this was actually against one of the five MiG-15s which the Soviets recorded as being damaged, rather than destroyed, during the action. The final force of 19 B-29s from the 98th BG was fortunate in that most of the MiG-15s were on the ground rearming and refueling when they reached the target area, so they were unmolested. However, the loss of six bombers, plus another that had crashed on landing at Kadena, was a rate of attrition that FEAF could not afford, and as a result of what was known as 'Black Thursday,' daylight deep penetration raids by B-29s were discontinued for the time being.

The last TARZON mission was flown on April 20, when a B-29 exploded shortly after attempting to jettison its TARZON weapon. Thirty TARZONs had been dropped operationally, of which just 12 were controllable, giving an overall success rate of 43 percent, but this average rate does not truly reflect the increasing accuracy after the weapons had been reworked and experience had been gained by maintenance and aircrews. The RAZON/TARZON campaign officially stopped in May 1951. By that time, the Chinese and North Koreans had started the construction of no less than eight bypass bridges to the main railway bridge at Sinuiju, which itself was still standing.

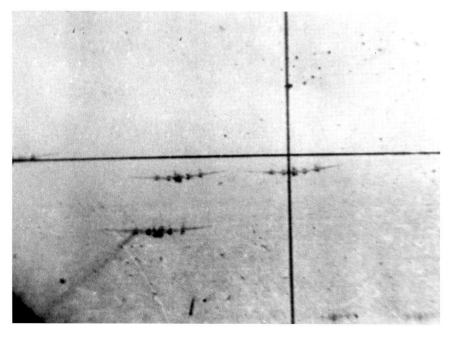

Gun camera film from a MiG-15 flown by Sen Lt Kochegarov from the 196th IAP (324th IAD) engaging a formation of B-29s near Sinuiju on April 12, 1951. Smoke is visible from the leftmost B-29 engine, which had been previously attacked by the leader, Capt Ivanov. (Krylov & Tepsurkaev)

B-29 Superfortresses of the 30th BS/19th BG on a daytime strike over North Korea in early 1951. The aircraft in the foreground was severely damaged by a MiG-15 on April 12, 1951, while bombing the railway bridge over Yalu River at Sinuiju and diverted to Seoul. (US National Archive)

Relieved of some of their close support tasks, the aircraft of TF 77 became available for interdiction missions in early March. Their targets were the railway tracks and bridges in Zones 'G' to 'H' on the eastern side of the country. The experiences of the naval aviators of CVG-19, flying from USS *Princeton* (CV-37), against a small bridge near Kilchu (Kilju) during March and April typifies the nature of the interdiction campaign. Just to the south of Kilchu, some 60 miles south of Chongjon, the rail line ran through a tunnel before crossing a 600ft-long bridge over a steep-sided valley. A parallel tunnel and bridge for an adjacent twin track were also under construction. The bridge was identified by a photo-reconnaissance sortie on March 2 and attacked the next day by eight Skyraiders of VA-195, armed with 2,000lb bombs. The sortie, led by Lt Cdr Harold G. Carlson, successfully destroyed one span and damaged three others; thereafter, the valley became known as 'Carlson's Canyon.' Repairs to the bridge started almost immediately, and despite repeated harassment by CVG-19 aircraft, it was almost ready to reopen two weeks later. An attack by 20 Skyraiders on March 15 destroyed the bridge once again, only for it to be repaired in the following fortnight. Although the bridge was completely destroyed in a strike by Skyraiders from USS *Princeton* and *Boxer* (CV-21) on April 2, the line was only disrupted for two months in total, since by May the North Koreans had completed a 4-mile bypass around the canyon.

It was a similar story on the other side of the country when B-29s destroyed a bypass to the railway bridge over the Chongchon River on April 1. Two weeks later, the bypass was in use again until it was successfully attacked once more by B-29s on April 24, but by then a second bypass was almost complete. Both structures were put out of action by another B-29 strike on May 2, but repairs to those bridges and the construction of other bypasses swiftly followed. By the end of the year, there were four railway bridges across the Chongchon River at Sinanju.

'Dambusters,' airfields and 'Black Tuesday'

By the end of April 1951, UNC forces had been pushed back from the Imjin River and held a front line running eastward from just north of Seoul. This included the lower reaches of the Pukhan River, a tributary of the Han, the flow of which was regulated by the Hwachon Dam. The dam itself was controlled by the CPVA/KPA, and UNC commanders feared that the Chinese and North Koreans could either flood the river to prevent UNC forces from crossing it or alternatively stop the flow and empty the river to permit their own forces to attack across it. After a UNC army operation to destroy the sluice gates on the dam failed in its objective, TF 77 was given the urgent task to disable the sluice gates on April 30. Although partial destruction of the sluice gates would release some water into the river, it would deny the Chinese the ability to control the flow in the river. That afternoon, six Skyraiders from VA-195, loaded with 2,000lb bombs and supported by five Corsairs to suppress the anti-aircraft defences, launched from USS *Princeton* and made an attempt to destroy the sluice gates, but their efforts were unsuccessful. The following morning, Cdr Richard C. Merrick led five Skyraiders from VA-195 and another three from CV-35 in another attempt on the dam. This time each aircraft was armed with a Mk-21 torpedo. Twelve Corsairs suppressed the AAA sites as the Skyraiders made their attacks from low over the reservoir. Two of the torpedoes did not guide, but the remaining six all hit the dam accurately, destroying one sluice gate, severely damaging another, and earning VA-195 the soubriquet 'The Dambusters.'

During the summer months, the majority of FEAF's effort was in response to requests for tactical support from the Army; however, Bomber Command also carried out strikes on the rail infrastructure and airfields in North Korea. On May 7, the 98th BG bombed the strategically important railway marshalling yards in Pyongyang. The B-29s were met with heavy AAA fire and two of the bombers were hit. 'Fireball' (44-62281) was able to return to Yokota Air Base, but 'Shady Lady' (44-86371), flown by Lt Col Vance E. Black, was shot down over the target; Black bailed out and was taken prisoner, but the other members of his crew were posted 'missing in action.' During May, the North Koreans demolished selected buildings in the city center in order to create a clearing in which they constructed a 7,000ft runway, easily long enough for jet aircraft. This airstrip was bombed, as was another at Yongyu, some 25 miles to the northwest, by B-29s from the 19th and 307th BGs on May 28. Four days later, the railway bridge at Kwaksan (Gwaksan), some 30 miles west of Sinanju, was attacked by 11 B-29s of the 98th BGs. The F-86 escorts were engaged by MiG-15s from

The Hwachon reservoir dam under attack by AD Skyraiders of VA-195 from USS *Princeton* (CV-37) on May 1, 1951. This attack, using torpedoes, successfully destroyed one floodgate and partially destroyed another, after earlier attempts to deny the CPLA/KPA the tactical use of controlled flooding on the Pukhan and Han Rivers by bombing the floodgates had failed. (US National Archive)

An AD-4 Skyraider of VA-195 prepares for a mission from USS *Princeton* in May 1951. (US National Archive)

the 18th GvIAP, who were on their first operational sortie. During this dogfight, one Soviet pilot, Sen Lt E. M. Stel'makh, saw the B-29s and broke away to attack them. Stel'makh shot down the Superfortress flown by Capt Joseph L. Korstjens, which was lost with its crew, and managed to damage one more before being shot down himself by F-86 pilot Capt Richard Ramsbottom of the 336th FIS. The damaged Superfortress, 'TDY Widow' (44-86335), made a successful emergency landing at Taegu.

The 'Downtown Pyongyang' airstrip was attacked again on July 3. In an indication of the level of threat now facing UNC aircraft over North Korea, this time the bomber force of six B-29s was supported by no less than 32 F-84s to suppress the AAA defences and another 33 F-86 escort fighters. Another six B-29s from the 19th BG bombed the airfield at Sinanju six days later, again with a heavy fighter escort. This time the bombers were intercepted by MiG-15s from the 10th and 12th Fighter Regiments of the PLAAF. Despite the efforts of the F-86 escorts, some MiG-15s were able to engage the bombers, but the only casualty was the Chinese regimental commander, Zhao Dahai, who was shot down into the Taedong estuary.

In early October, the main concern of FEAF commanders was the discovery of three large airfields that were being built in the vicinity of Sinanju. The airfield at Saamchan had been constructed alongside the Chongchon River at Kaechon, 15 miles northeast of Sinanju, while that at Taechon was situated in a loop of the Taeryong River about 20 miles north of Sinanju. The third airfield, Namsi, was at Panghyon, some 15 miles west of Taechon. If these airfields became operational, they could potentially be used as forward bases for MiG-15s, in which case PLAAF and KPAF aircraft would be able to reach as far south as Pyongyang and the airspace north of the city would become as hotly contested as that in 'MiG Alley.' Given the threat of Antung-based MiG-15s during daylight, the initial plan for neutralizing the airfields was to bomb them at night using the SHORAN system that had been re-established earlier in the year. Unfortunately, night raids against Saamchan on October 13 and 14 were not a success, highlighting the practical problem with using SHORAN in an area where mapping coverage was not particularly accurate.

After the failure of the night missions, it was clear that further attacks would have to be carried out during daylight in order to achieve sufficient bombing accuracy. Diversionary attacks by fighter-bombers against targets further to the north were planned to coincide with the B-29 strikes, to keep the MiG-15s away from the more vulnerable bombers, which in turn were also strongly escorted by F-84s. On October 18 and 21, the 98th BG missed its rendezvous with its escort, so rather than taking unnecessary risks, the bombers sensibly diverted instead to secondary targets south of the Chongchon River. However, the 19th BG carried out a successful mission against Saamchan on October 18 and was then tasked to strike Taechon on October 22. On this day, a force of nine B-29s with a close escort of F-84s reached Taechon under an overcast at about 19,000ft. While 40 MiG-15s which had been scrambled from Tatungkao engaged a fighter-bomber raid that was taking place to the north, 14 MiG-15s from the 18th GvIAP were vectored towards the B-29 raid. Descending in a mass formation through over 15,000ft of cloud, the MiG-15s, led by Lt Col A. P. Smorchkov, burst out from the overcast and caught the B-29s just after they had dropped their bombs. One B-29, 'Cream of the Crop' (44-61656), flown by Capt Lyle B. Bordeaux, had already been damaged by antiaircraft fire, and the MiG attack disabled two of its engines. The bomber crew bailed out over the Yellow Sea. The bombing attack against Taechon had been very successful, but the accurate AAA fire and the attack by the MiG-15s had provided a foretaste of what was to come.

The third airfield, at Namsi, was attacked on October 23, a day that became known as 'Black Tuesday'. The 307th BG was tasked for the mission that morning, and nine B-29s, in three flights – Able, Baker and Charlie – each of three bombers, set out from Okinawa, bound for the target. After they crossed the front lines, they linked up with their fighter escort of 24 F-84s provided by the 49th and 136th FBGs. A fighter screen of 31 F-86s also patrolled a line between Sonchon and Kusong (Guseong) to keep MiG-15s away from the bombers. Because of the likelihood of cloud obscuring the target, the attack on Namsi had been planned to follow a SHORAN profile, but this routing led the bombers directly over the target of the previous day at Taechon, with its formidable AAA batteries. As they overflew Taechon, some of the bombers were damaged by AAA fire, but after leaving the gun engagement zone they became vulnerable to fighter attack. Soviet air defence radars had already detected the raid, and the MiG-15s of the 303rd IAD were launched to intercept. Shortly after the three regimental formations – consisting of 20 MiG-15s from the 17th

IAP, 20 from the 18th GvIAP, and 18 from the 523rd IAP – headed towards Namsi, two regiments of the 324th IAD also launched with another 26 MiG-15s, as a second wave. Splitting the MiG-15 force to keep the F-86 screen tied up, the Soviet fighters swept down through the F-84 escort and wreaked havoc amongst the B-29s just after the first flight of bombers, Able Flight, had dropped their weapon load. In Able Flight, the Number 3 aircraft (42-94045), flown by Capt Robert R. Krumm, was shot down, most probably by Lt Col Smorchkov of the 18th GvIAP, and the other two B-29s in the flight were both badly damaged. The Able Flight lead aircraft, 'Sit N Git' (44-69816), flown by Capt Clarence Fogler, was

Bombs explode on the newly constructed airfield at Saamchan on the banks of the Chongchon River during a raid by B-29 Superfortresses on October 18, 1951. (NMUSAF)

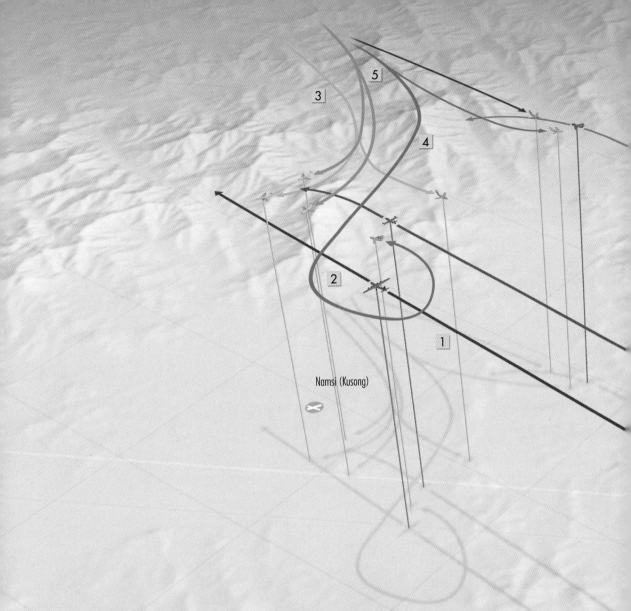

Namsi (Kusong)

EVENTS

1 0840hrs Able Flight B-29s pass Taechon and are engaged by the anti-aircraft defences.

2 0843hrs Able Flight B-29s release bombs on Namsi airfield.

3 0844hrs MiG-15s of 18 GvIAP attack Able Flight. The Number 3 B-29 (42-94045) flown by Capt Robert R. Krumm is shot down by a MiG-15 and the other two bombers are badly damaged.

4 0845hrs MiG-15s of 523rd IAP attack Baker and Charlie Flight B-29s. The third aircraft of Baker flight

(44-61940), flown by Capt James A. Foulkes, which had been badly hit by AAA over Taechon, is shot down by a MiG-15. Both of the remaining bombers in Baker Flight are so badly damaged that they have to divert to Kimpo. In the third section, Charlie Flight, one B-29 (44-70151) flown by Capt Thomas L. Shields is also shot down by a MiG-15.

5 0846hrs MiG-15s of 17 IAP attack Able Flight B-29s. After sustaining heavy damage, Able Flight lead aircraft, 'Sit N Git' (44-69816) flown by Capt Clarence Fogler, is forced to divert to Kimpo.

Namsi Raid

The airfield at Namsi was attacked on October 23, 'Black Tuesday'. That morning, nine B-29s of the 19th BG, in three flights of three, set out from Okinawa, bound for the target. They were protected by a fighter escort of 24 F-84s and a fighter screen of 31 F-86s.

Capt James A. Foulkes

Capt Robert R. Krumm

Capt Thomas L. Shields

B-29 Bomber Formation

Taechon

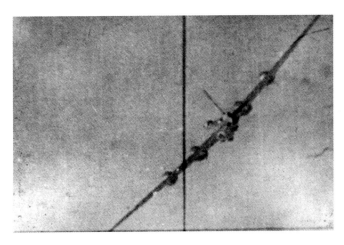

MiG-15 gun camera film of the attack by Lt Col A. P. Smorchkov from the 18th GvIAP (303rd IAD) against B-29s near Taechon on October 23, 1951. (Krylov & Tepsurkaev)

forced to divert to Kimpo; after it had landed, the bomber was found to have 500 shell holes in it. The second section of bombers, Baker Flight, fared even worse: the leading aircraft (44-61940), flown by Capt James A. Foulkes, which had been badly hit by AAA over Taechon, was then shot down by a MiG-15, probably flown by Maj D. P. O'skin of the 523rd IAP, whose cannon fire set an engine alight. Most of the crew had bailed out by the time the aircraft exploded. Both of the remaining Superfortresses in Baker Flight were so badly damaged that they had to divert to Kimpo. The third section, Charlie Flight, also lost one B-29 (44-70151), flown by Capt Thomas L. Shields, probably another victim of Maj O'skin. The remaining aircraft in Charlie Flight were relatively lightly damaged and were able to return to their base. During the engagements, one of the escorting F-84s had also been shot down and three MiG-15s had been damaged. In the following days, there were more daylight B-29 raids, but it was already clear that future daylight operations would result in a prohibitively high attrition rate.

The targets for the last three daylight missions were the bridges at Sunchon, Sinanju and Songchon (Seoncheon). On October 24, eight B-29s from the 98th BG escorted by 16 Meteors and ten F-84s bombed the highway bridge at Sunchon. Once again, the three MiG-15 regiments of the 303rd IAD launched en-masse and 55 MiG-15s headed towards the bombers. The Soviet pilots repeated the tactics of the previous day, with the 20 MiG-15s of the 523rd IAP tasked with tying up the F-86 screen while the other MiGs attacked the B-29s. The MiGs had only just caught up with the bombers before they crossed the coast near Wonsan, and since the Soviet pilots were prohibited from flying over the sea, they only managed one attacking pass. Nevertheless, Lt Col A. P. Smorchkov of the 18th GvIAP shot down his third B-29 victim in three days, 'Our Gal,' flown by 1st Lt Luke C. Fyffe, although in doing so he was wounded by the defensive fire from the bomber. Two other B-29s were also damaged. Three days later, another eight B-29s from the 19th BG, accompanied again by 16 Meteors and 32 F-84s, raided the railway bridge at Sinanju. Once again, the formation was attacked by a strong force of Soviet fighters: 40 MiG-15s from the 17th and 18th GvIAPs engaged the escort fighters, while Maj A. N. Karasev led 22 MiG-15s from the 303rd IAP against the bombers. One B-29, flown by Capt Vito J. Fiero, was damaged and had to carry out an emergency landing at Seoul (K-14), and two others were less seriously damaged. During the engagement, the gunners of 'Command Decision' (44-87657), a B-29 flown by Capt Donald M. Covic, claimed their fifth MiG kill. A raid against Songchon the next day was unchallenged, but the decision was taken that day by FEAF commanders to limit the B-29 in future to night operations.

Midway through October, a US intelligence source in North Korea, known as Unit Y, indicated that senior Chinese and North Korean military staff would be holding a conference at Kapsan, a small village in the mountainous area of northeast Korea, at the end of the month. TF 77 was given the task of attacking the conference venue and thereby neutralizing the senior leadership of the CPVA and KPA. On October 29, Cdr Paul N. Gray led a strike force comprising four Banshees, eight Corsairs and eight Skyraiders from USS Essex (CV-9), and four Panthers, eight Corsairs and eight Skyraiders from USS Antietam (CV-36). The role of the Panthers and Banshees was to attack the known AAA batteries with rockets before the Corsairs followed them to drop airburst-fused bombs on any batteries that were still active. The main strike force of Skyraiders was armed with

1,000lb bombs and napalm, and its target was the 16 buildings in a barrack area on the outskirts of Kapsan. Although it was met with intensive antiaircraft fire, the entire strike force made six runs across the site from different directions to ensure the destruction of all the buildings, leaving the compound a smoking ruin. Unit Y agents later reported that over 500 senior personnel had been killed in the compound and that the records of the North Korean Communist Party had been destroyed.

Night Bombing (1)

Nightly raids by B-29s against North Korean airfields commenced on November 4. With only a limited number of SHORAN transceivers, these sorties were flown by between five and seven aircraft each night and it was accepted that the attacks would not be very accurate. Meanwhile, FEAF made efforts to procure and fit SHORAN transceivers in all of its bombers and to give training to both the aircrews and ground station operators. More accurate mapping based on aerial photographs was also produced. During November 1951, 26 sorties were flown against Namsi, 23 against Taechon, and 12 each against Saamchan and Uiju. At the first three locations, the aim was to crater the runways and put them beyond use, whereas at Uiju the bombers dropped airburst 500lb bombs to target aircraft parked on the dispersal areas. It also became clear at this time that North Korean ingenuity had re-established bridges at Sunchon, Sianju and Pyongyang. A bypass bridge at Sunchon appeared to be disused because two spans were missing, but it was discovered that the North Koreans were removing them by day and reinstating them at night to allow traffic to use the bridge in the hours of darkness. At Sinanju, the road bridge was repaired, while a bypass bridge had been built at Pyongyang. All three bridges were bombed at the end of the month, but the bridges at Sunchon were not hit and those at Sinanju could not be put out of operation for any longer than two-day periods.

In response to the night-bombing campaign, the CPVA/KPA began to site more AAA guns and searchlights at the airfields and along the SHORAN approach paths to them. However, despite this development, only five bombers were damaged during November. In December, Soviet night fighters also started to operate near the Yalu River, and B-29s were damaged in night-fighter attacks on December 4 and 23.

By the end of 1951, most B-29s were operating mainly by night. This aircraft of the 98th BG is wearing the black camouflage scheme that was adopted for night missions. (US National Archive)

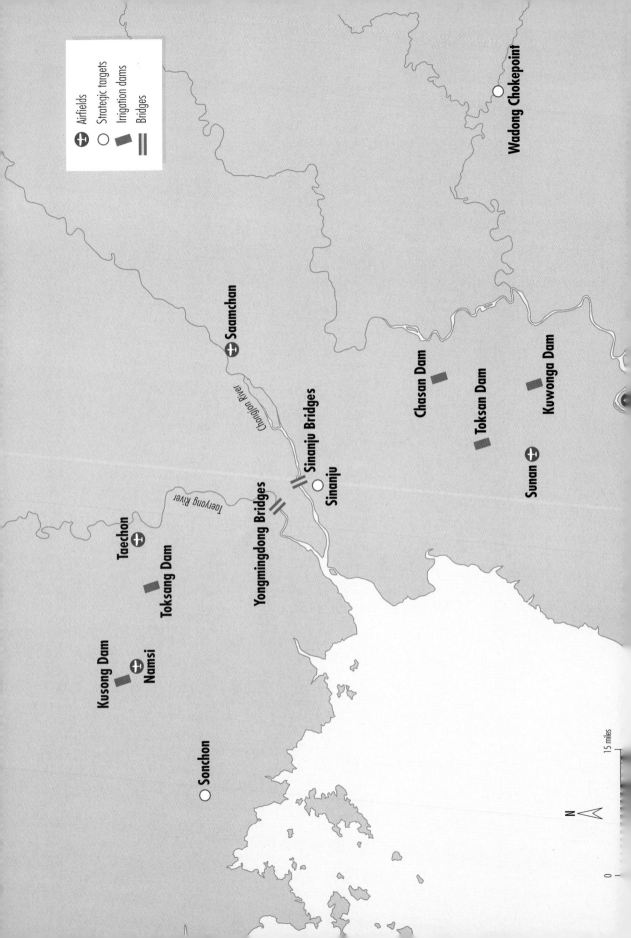

Airfields

Strategic targets

Irrigation dams

Bridges

Wadong Chokepoint

Saamchan

Chongjon River

Chasan Dam

Toksan Dam

Kuwonga Dam

Sinanju Bridges

Sunan

Sinanju

Taeryong River

Yongmingdong Bridges

Taechon

Toksang Dam

Kusong Dam

Namsi

Sonchon

N

0   15 miles

OPPOSITE BRIDGES AND IRRIGATION DAMS 1953

In early 1953, UNC aircraft participated in two campaigns – firstly against the bridges crossing the Chongjon River at Sinanju and the Taeryong River at Yongmidong, and secondly against the irrigation reservoirs to the north of Pyongyang. This map also shows the location of the Wadong Chokepoint, which was the target of a short interdiction campaign in early 1952.

The mountainous terrain of North Korea dictated that the main road and rail systems ran inland of the east and west coastlines, and were separated by the central highlands; however, they were linked by a lateral east–west arm that ran from Pyongyang to Wonsan, through the lower ground at Songchon and Yangdok. In early January 1952, FEAF planners noticed a chokepoint in both the rail and road systems near the village of Wadong, 10 miles northwest of Yangdok. Here, the main highway from Wonsan to Pyongyang crossed the lateral railway line as they threaded through a deep river gorge. Target planners at FEAF believed this to be the ideal point to cut off both road and rail communications: it seemed that any bombs that fell into a 750ft length of the gorge could not fail to miss either the road or the rail track. Furthermore, they believed that this result could be achieved by 'saturation bombing' at night using SHORAN. In a sustained effort in the 44 days between January and March 11, B-29s and B-26s dropped nearly 4,000 500lb bombs into the gorge. A total of 77 B-29 and 125 B-26 sorties were flown during the campaign, but the results were disappointing: only 18 cuts of the rail track and 15 cuts of the roadway were achieved, and at best the railway was blocked for just seven days and the road for just four days. The rest of the bombs had done little but churn up the surrounding countryside.

At the same time that it became apparent that attacking the chokepoint would not provide the expected results, it was clear, too, that the tactical interdiction program codenamed Operation *Strangle* was also failing and that a different approach was needed. This was Operation *Saturate*, which started on March 3, 1952, in which the strategic bombers were to concentrate on the strategically important Sunchon and Sinanju bridge complexes. The Sinanju complex comprised a rail bridge and a road bridge plus five rail bypass bridges across the Chonchon River, along with a further five bridges across the Taeryong River some 3 miles to the north. Some spans were cut in a raid by 47 B-29s on March 28, just three days after 41 B-29s had made nine cuts in bridges at Pyongyang. On March 31, 13 B-29s bombed the railway bridge at Sinhung (approximately 15 miles north of Hamhung). Throughout May, B-29s cut 66 spans from ten bridges.

The joint Soviet, Chinese and North Korean night-fighting capability had been steadily improving as the night-bombing campaign continued through the first half of 1952. On the night of June 10, 11 B-29s from the 19th BG were tasked to hit the complex of railway bridges at Kwaksan. It was a clear night, and over the target the first ten bombers in the stream were all coned by searchlights and met by both heavy AAA fire and fighter attacks. In response to radar warning of the raid, two pairs of MiG-15s were scrambled. Lt Col M. I. Studilin, commander of the 147th GvIAP, engaged the Superfortress 'Miss Jackie the Rebel' (44-61967), flown by Maj George A. Hadley, as it was held by the searchlights and shot it down; the crew did not survive. Shortly afterwards, also locating his targets when they were illuminated by the searchlights, Capt A. M. Karelin from the 351st IAP attacked two bombers: 'Hot to Go' (44-62183), flown by Capt Louis P. Gorrell, exploded over the target, while 'Apache' (44-61902), flown by Capt George Perry, was so badly damaged by Karelin that it was forced to divert to Kimpo (K-14). The 11th bomber in the stream used its ECM and was able to escape the attentions of the searchlights and fighters. This raid had emphasized the need for some degree of fighter support for future night-bomber operations.

The Chosin Number 3 hydroelectric generator station – an extract from USAF target listing. Each of the four stations in the system comprised the cylindrical surge tank at the top of the hill, from which the penstocks led water to the generators in the powerhouse; the switching and distribution gear is on the right of the powerhouse. (US National Archive)

KOREA AREAS NOS. 84.1, 2, 3, 4, 5, 6, 7, 8 GENERAL PHOTOS (KONAN REGION)   **DESCRIPTION OF TARGETS**

CONFIDENTIAL equals British Confidential

LOOKING NW

DATE UNKNOWN

PHOTO 42—Choshin Hydro-electric Plant No. 3 (Not listed as a target).

'Air Pressure'

During their occupation of Korea, the Japanese had built an impressive network of hydroelectric power stations, which provided electrical power not only to the whole of North Korea but also a large part of southern Manchuria. They were built on the Suiho (Supung), Chosin (Changjin), Fusen (Pujon) and Kyosen (Pungsan) reservoirs. The 300-megawatt power station on the Suiho dam, some 40 miles upstream of Sinuiju, was the fourth-largest hydroelectric plant in the world: a conventional design, it drew water from the Suiho reservoir on the Yalu River to drive four generators in a powerhouse at the foot of the dam. However, the Changjin, Fusen and Kyosen dams were of an ingeniously unconventional design. In these systems, where the reservoirs were high in the relatively gentle western slopes of the mountains, rather than feeding the water through the dams, the Japanese engineers had directed it via tunnels through the watershed to the steeper slopes on the eastern side, where it was channeled through penstocks connecting a series of generating stations built into the hillsides. Each of these systems consisted of a chain of four generating stations stretched over a distance of between 10 and 30 miles.

The power network had been identified as a possible target in 1950, and the Fusen Number 1 plant had been bombed by the 92nd BG on September 26, 1950; but it was not until the summer of 1952 that a large-scale strike was planned against the whole network. The aim of the attack was to apply strategic pressure on the North Korean delegation at the armistice negotiations at Panmunjom. The ambitious plan to strike all four generating systems in the network simultaneously would require fighter-bombers from all the combat arms in the theatre and would need close coordination. The attacks by USAF and USMC aircraft would have to be deconflicted from and coordinated with aircraft operating from the four aircraft carriers of TF 77.

The attack was originally planned for the morning of June 23, but poor weather over the target area delayed the strike until 1600hrs. At that time, 84 F-86s were patrolling the Yalu River to ensure that no MiG-15s could interfere with the attack on the Suiho dam. The first aircraft over the target were 36 Panthers drawn from USS *Boxer* (CV-21), *Philippine Sea* and *Princeton*, which attacked the AAA sites around the dam; they were followed by

35 Skyraiders from the same ships which hit the powerhouse with 2,000lb bombs. Shortly afterwards, a follow-up attack was carried out by 79 F-84s from the 49th and 136th FBGs and 45 Lockheed F-80 Shooting Stars from the 8th FBG. In a short space of time, some 230 tons of bombs had been dropped onto the Suiho plant. At the same time, 39 Panthers and 45 Corsairs from the 1st Marine Air Wing bombed the Chosin Numbers 3 and 4 generator stations, while North American F-51 Mustangs of the 18th FBG struck the Fusen Numbers 3 and 4 stations. Fusen Number 2 and Kyosen Number 2 were hit by Skyraiders and Corsairs from USS *Bon Homme Richard* (CV-31), Kyosen Number 3 by aircraft from USS *Princeton*, and Kyosen Number 4 by aircraft from USS *Boxer*. All of the attacks were successful and, thanks to poor weather over Antung and the presence of large-scale F-86 patrols, no MiG-15s attempted to intervene. There was spirited AAA fire near some targets, but it was effectively limited by dedicated defence-suppression aircraft. One Corsair from USS *Boxer*, flown by Lt Cdr W. S. Miller, was damaged by AAA over Kyosen 4 but successfully ditched, while a Skyraider from USS *Bon Homme Richard* was hit by flying concrete after scoring a direct hit on the Fusen Number 2 generator house.

The hydroelectric system was also targeted the following day. TF 77 aircraft bombed the Fusen Numbers 1 and 2 and Kyosen Numbers 3 and 4 plants, while fighter-bombers from the 8th, 18th and 136th FBGs attacked the Chosin Numbers 1 and 2 and Fusen Number 4 plants. Further attacks on the Chosin and Fusen systems were mounted by the 8th, 18th and 136th FBGs on June 26, targeting other parts of the electrical distribution infrastructure, and on June 27 the 49th and 136th FBGs struck once again at Chosin Numbers 1 and 2 plants. The campaign resulted in a major loss of electrical power throughout North Korea and Manchuria, with an almost total blackout in Korea for two weeks and the loss of 23 percent of the electricity requirement in northeast China.

Further 'Air Pressure' was applied by UNC tactical aircraft in early July. On July 4, 70 fighter-bombers attacked the North Korean Military Academy at Sakchu, 7 miles southeast of the Suiho dam, but although the raid was unopposed, the bombing was not accurate.

A Grumman F9F Panther of VMF-311 of the US Marine Corps at Pohang in December 1950. These aircraft were tasked to strike the Chosin Number 3 and 4 generator stations during the 'Powerplant Raids' on June 23, 1952. (US National Archive)

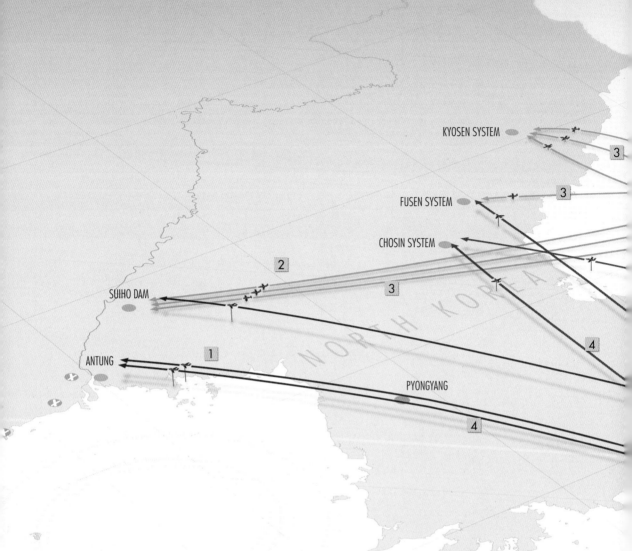

KYOSEN SYSTEM

FUSEN SYSTEM

CHOSIN SYSTEM

3

3

2

3

SUIHO DAM

4

1

ANTUNG

PYONGYANG

NORTH KOREA

4

EVENTS

1 1600hrs 40 F-86 Sabres from 4th and 51st FIGs carry out a pre-strike fighter sweep at 25,000ft. 20 F-86 Sabres from 4th FIG establish a Combat Air Patrol over Antung at 18,000ft. VVS and CPLAAF MiG-15s are unable to take-off.

2 1610hrs F9F Panthers from USS *Boxer*, USS *Philippine Sea* and USS *Princeton* target the anti aircraft defences while AD Skyraiders from USS *Boxer* attack the Suiho power station generator building.

3 1615hrs F4U Corsairs and AD Skyraiders from USS *Bon Homme Richard* and USS *Boxer* attack Fusen 2. F4U Corsairs and AD Skyraiders from USS *Bon Homme Richard* and USS *Boxer* attack Kyosen 2.

F4U Corsairs and AD Skyraiders from USS *Princeton* attack Kyosen 3 with F9F from USS *Bon Homme Richard*. AD Skyraiders from USS *Princeton* and USS *Philippine Sea* carry out follow-up attacks on the Suiho generator building.

4 1625hrs–1700hrs 45 F-80 Shooting Stars from 8th FBG and 79 F-84 Thunderjets from 49th and 136th FBG attack Suiho. F-51 Mustangs from 18th FBG attack Fusen 3 and 4. F9F Panthers from MAG-33 attack Fusen 1 and 2. F4U Corsairs from MAG-12 attack Chosin 3 and 4. 25 F-86s Sabres from 4th and 51st FIGs and two RF-80s carry out post-strike reconnaissance.

Power station raid: the attacks on 23 June, 1952

On 23 June, 1952, 500 aircraft were tasked to destroy the hydro-electric power-generation network in North Korea to pressurise the North Korean delegation at the Armistice negotiations into making concessions.

The Chosin Number 3 hydroelectric generator station after the 'Powerplant Raids' in June 1952. Compare this with the previous image. The powerhouse has been wrecked and the penstocks have been completely severed. (US National Archive)

Four days later, 84 fighter-bombers attacked bridges on the railway line between Kanggye and Kunu-ri, while 41 others attacked Chosin Numbers 1 and 2 generator plants once again. Meanwhile, the 'Air Pressure' concept had developed into Operation *Pressure Pump*, a coordinated effort to mount mass airstrikes, integrating the air superiority, interdiction, and air support tasks into a single mission using overwhelming force. This latest iteration of the FEAF and TF 77 interdiction plans commenced on July 11 with a series of three large-scale strikes throughout the day against 30 targets in the Pyongyang area. Naval aircraft from the carriers USS *Bon Homme Richard* and *Princeton* joined in these raids, but poor weather in the Sea of Japan meant that instead of refueling and rearming on their carriers, they had to divert to air force bases in South Korea and were unable to participate in the second and third waves. In all, some 1,254 sorties were flown during the day, including 54 SHORAN-directed attacks by B-29s that night. The bombers attacked eight targets which were supply and storage depots or factories.

Follow-up raids against the power supply system were also mounted to disrupt repair efforts to the generators and transformers. The Chosin Number 3 generator station was

bombed by Skyraiders and Corsairs from USS *Bon Homme Richard* and *Princeton* on July 19, and the Chosin Number 2 station was also hit by 44 B-29s on the nights of July 19 and 21. During August, aircraft operating from USS *Essex* attacked the Kyosen Numbers 1 and 2 and Chosin Number 1 plants.

The remaining North Korea industrial infrastructure was also targeted during the summer. The Sungho-ri cement plant had been bombed by a large force of 171 fighter-bombers from 5th AF on July 15, and the lead and zinc mill at Sindok and magnesite plant at Kilchu were struck by naval aircraft respectively from USS *Bon Homme Richard* on July 27 and *Princeton* the following day. Then, on July 30, the Oriental Light Metal Company in Sinuiju was the target for the largest strategic night-bomber raid of the war, when it was bombed by a force of 63 B-29s. Directed by SHORAN, the bombers dropped their bombloads through a low overcast which also frustrated the efforts of the Chinese and North Korean searchlight operators, enabling the bomber force to complete its attack without loss.

The pressure was maintained throughout August, including large-scale fighter-bomber attacks on a tungsten mine at Kilju and a chemical plant at Inhung-ni. On August 18, 14 B-29s bombed the Nakwon Munitions Plant, a grenade factory to the southeast of Sinuiju. However, the most important event of the month was Operation *Pressure Pump 2*, which took place on August 29. Once again, 5th AF fighter-bombers were joined by naval strike aircraft to mount three massive air attacks against targets in the Pyongyang area during the course of the day. F-84s from the 474th FBG and F-80s from the 8th FBG attacked AAA emplacements before the first wave, which concentrated on government and military buildings, as well as warehouses and factories. The following night, a follow-up raid by 11 B-29s from the 19th BG completed the task.

Demonstrating its ability to reach far into North Korea, TF 77 carried out the largest naval strike of the war on September 1. Lying in the far northeast of Korea and just 8 miles from the border with the USSR, the synthetic oil facility at Aoji was well beyond the range of the 5th AF fighter-bombers and too close to the border to be attacked by B-29s. It was also beyond the range of the MiG-15s and, probably because the North Koreans believed it to be safe from attack, it was undefended by AAA. While aircraft from USS *Boxer* carried out diversionary attacks at Chongjin and Munsan, USS *Essex* and *Princeton* launched their aircraft towards Aoji. With no AAA or fighter threat at Aoji, the strike aircraft were able to make repeated bombing runs to ensure the destruction of their target.

Night Bombing (2)

Early September saw attacks on some previously struck targets. On September 9, 82 F-84s, escorted by F-86s, bombed the North Korean Air Force Academy at Sakchu once more. This time the bombing was more accurate, but the defences were also more effective. The F-84s were intercepted by a large force of MiG-15s from the 133rd and 216th IAD, which shot down two F-84s and an F-80, and caused many other UNC aircraft to jettison their ordnance before they could complete their attack. But the Soviets paid a high price for their success: six MiG-15s were shot down by the F-86 screen and three Soviet pilots were killed. After reports that two generators at the Suiho dam were still operational, another attempt was made to neutralize the power station, this time by B-29s. Just before midnight on September 12, six B-29s started dropping aluminium foil strips to jam the enemy radars, and six B-26s attacked searchlights, successfully extinguishing 30 of them. However, some searchlights were based on the northern side of the Yalu River and were therefore immune from attack and, though deprived of their radar, the anti-aircraft batteries continued to fire a heavy box-barrage. Two MiG-15 night fighters were scrambled to intercept the bombing force, and Sen Lt Y. Dobrovichan fired on the B-29 'Wolf Pack' (44-86343) of the 307th BG, flown by Capt James A. Lowe, which exploded over the target area. The unforgiving nature of the weather over Korea was emphasized when another bomber, 'Bait Me' (44-69802), of the 19th BG, flown by Capt John L. Roberts, crashed during the return leg after encountering severe icing, although the crew was safely recovered. Unfortunately, despite causing extensive damage to the complex, the bombers failed to hit the generator building.

UNC F-84 fighter-bomber groups were also involved in strategic strikes in mid-September. On September 15, Col Victor E. Warford led 24 F-84s from the 58th FBG to attack the port and supply depot at Sinuiju. The escorting F-86s successfully kept the MiG-15s away

A pilot of the 9th FBS/49th FBG straps into an F-84G Thunderjet armed with 1,000lb Mk 65 bombs at Taegu (K-2). This aircraft was shot down by MiG-15s on September 9, 1952; the pilot, Capt Warren E. O'Brien, was posted 'Missing in Action.' (US National Archive)

from the strike force, so that despite the proximity of the target to the Antung complex, there were no losses amongst the F-84s. The following week, on September 21, it was the turn of Col William W. Ingenhutt to lead 41 F-84s from the 474th FBG against the munitions factory at Pukchong (Bukcheong) on the east coast (45 miles northeast of Hamhung) for another successful strike. The poor weather at the end of September provided ideal cover for a B-29 night SHORAN attack on the Namsan-ni chemical plant on the banks of the Yalu River near the Suiho reservoir. Repeating the tactics tried earlier in the month, three B-29s dropped proximity-fused bombs over anti-aircraft positions and then orbited the area while jamming enemy radar signals, while seven B-26s attacked searchlights. The main force of 45 B-29s then dropped their bombs, successfully destroying the plant.

Reflecting the improved relations between the USAF and USN, a coordinated daylight airstrike was conducted on October 8 against the important rail junction at Kowon (Gowon), some 20 miles north of Wonsan on the east coast. Ten B-29s escorted by Banshees from

The wreckage of B-29 'Wolf Pack' (44-86343) of the 307th BG, flown by Capt James A. Lowe, which exploded over the Suiho dam after it was shot down by Sen Lt Y. Dobrovichan on the night of September 12, 1952. (Krylov & Tepsurkaev)

AD Skyraiders (VA-65) dive bomb the Suiho dam generating station, 23 June, 1952

An AD-4 Skyraider, BuNo 123820 from VA-65, which launched from USS *Boxer*, recovers from its dive-bombing attack against the hydro-electric power station on the Suiho Dam. The aircraft is climbing through 4,000ft over the Suiho reservoir, while other Skyraiders make their attacks behind it. A mass attack on the hydro-electric power stations in North Korea by Navy, Air Force and Marine Corps aircraft took place at 1600hrs on the afternoon of 23 June 1952. The AD-4 Skyraiders of VA-65 were tasked against the generator building at the foot of the Suiho dam (now known as the Supung dam). Each Skyraider delivered its load of two 2,000lb bombs, delivered from a 20° dive. F9F Panthers from the carriers USS *Boxer*, *Philippine Sea* and *Princeton* had attacked the anti-aircraft positions on the southern side of the Yalu River just prior to the attack by the Skyraiders. The same target was bombed a few minutes later by AD Skyraiders from USS *Princeton* and USS *Philippine Sea*, which were then followed by 45 F-80 Shooting Stars from 8th FBG and 79 F-84 Thunderjets from 49th and 136th FBG. Some 145 tons of bombs were dropped on the Suiho power station during the course of the attack.

VF-11, operating from USS *Kearsarge* (CV-33), bombed the antiaircraft batteries in the area, after which naval aircraft from USS *Kearsarge*, *Essex* and *Princeton* attacked bridges and railway installations.

Strategic operations during the winter of 1952–53 were limited by both poor weather and the lack of suitable targets. Nevertheless, the UNC leadership was determined to maintain the 'Air Pressure' during a two-month recess in the armistice talks, which had become deadlocked. FEAF Bomber Command mounted nightly raids by four or six aircraft whenever the weather permitted, to mop up any elements of industrial activity, transportation infrastructure or storage facilities. Night-bomber activity was now being supported by the SkyKnights of VMF(N)-513, and Cpt Oliver R. Davis and WO Dramus F. Fessler were credited with the first Skyknight MiG-15 kill on November 8; but interestingly, no corresponding loss is recorded by the Soviets and indeed Sen Lt I. P. Kovalev was credited with the damage or destruction of a Skyknight. It is possible that PLAAF aircraft were lost that night, but the incident demonstrates the difficulty in confirming kill claims at night. On November 12, six B-29s dropped four spans from the rail bridges at Pyongyang, and the following night the supply storage area at Sopo, on the northerly outskirts of Pyongyang, was also attacked by five bombers.

On November 17, the target was the mine at Choak-tong, to the east of Sinuiju, and on November 18, the 98th BG bombed the supply center at Sonchon. The latter raid was carried out under clear skies, and MiG-15s from both the 147th GvIAP and 532st IAP were patrolling the area. Both UNC bomber crews and Soviet fighter pilots reported afterwards that flares were being dropped to illuminate the sky, but each side thought it was the other. It seems possible, therefore, that PLAAF fighters were also airborne that night. Soon after dropping its bombs, B-29 'Wrights' Delights, They Chosen Flew' (44-86392), flown by Maj William F. Sawyer, was intercepted by Sen Lt Dobrovichan, of the 147th GvIAP, who shot it down. Two crew members managed to escape from the doomed bomber and were rescued, but the other 12 were killed.

A daylight raid by 117 F-84s damaged the Oryong-dong target complex, to the northeast of Chonju (Jeongju), on November 21. A week later, in a large-scale night raid on November 28,

44 B-29s flying in three waves bombed targets in Sinuiju and Uiju. Thanks to their protective measures, and despite clear skies, all of the bombers returned to base undamaged. However, the bombing at Uiju, as well as that at Choak-rong four nights previously, was not effective enough and both targets had to be reattacked. Fourteen B-29s from the 307th BG were dispatched to Uiju on the night of December 12, and in the last major action of the year on the night of December 30, six B-29s from the 19th BG bombed the ore processing plant at Choak-tong, while 12 B-29s were sent against targets in the Pakchong area. It was a clear night with bright moonlight, and contrails above 25,000ft. Five MiG-15s had been scrambled to intercept them, including Maj A. M. Karelin of the 351st IAP, who was instructed to hold over the Suiho reservoir. Following the contrails, Karelin engaged one of the last bombers in the stream, 44-62011, flown by 1st Lt Robert R. Foster. Karelin fired six separate bursts at it and saw the aircraft break up in front of him. On his return to Antung, parts of the B-29 were found embedded in the MiG-15. The other four MiG-15 pilots also carried out successful intercepts, damaging two more B-29s: 44-87596 was forced to divert to Suwon, while 'Lady in Dis-Dress' (44-86446) made an emergency landing at Tokyo. Two of the B-29s in the Pakchon area were also fired on.

The Sinanju and Yongmidong bridges

The main North Korean railway line running south from Sinuiju to Pyongyang was the double-track Kyongui (Gyeongui) Line which, built in the early 1900s, ran down the west coast. At Chongju, it was joined by a single-track line running from Namsan-ni (some 35 miles upstream along the Yalu River from Sinuiju). This main artery then crossed the Taeryong River at Yongmidong before running through a large switching and marshalling yard at Maengjungni and then crossing the Chongchon River at Sinanju. At the beginning of the war, each of the rivers had been crossed by a single large concrete and steel railway bridge and a parallel road bridge. The bridges over both rivers had been the targets of numerous attacks during 1951 and 1952, but the North Koreans had repaired damaged bridges and also constructed a fan of bypass crossings over each river to maintain the traffic flow. By late 1952,

Bomb-armed F-84s of the 474th FBG. Col William W. Ingenhutt led 41 aircraft from this unit against the munitions factory at Pukchong on the east coast of North Korea on September 21, 1952. (US National Archive)

The bridges over the Chongchon River at Sinanju under attack from B-29s in October 1952. The numerous bypass tracks and bridges can be clearly seen. (US National Archive)

bridges identified by the UNC as B-62, B-63, B-64 North and South, and B-65 crossed the Taeryong River, while B-66, B-67, B-73, B-74, B-75, and the road bridge D-68 spanned the Chongchon River. Another railway line, running south from Manpojin on the Chinese border, crossed the Chongchon River at Kunuri, some 15 miles upstream, near Saamchan airfield. From Sinanju and Kunuri, the supplies and materiel carried by the rail network were transferred from the main rail lines to other forms of transport, including trucks and pack animals, for transport southwards to the front. In this last leg of their journey, the loads were widely dispersed across the numerous tracks across the countryside and were therefore almost impossible to interdict; however, the 3½-mile stretch of rail track between the Taeryong and Chongchon Rivers formed a chokepoint in the network, and in January 1953, UNC air commanders decided to mount a concerted effort against it.

The aim of the campaign was twofold: firstly, to close down the western arm of the major resupply route from China permanently; and secondly, to demonstrate to the North Korean leadership the ability of the UNC to apply air pressure wherever it wished to do so by using its air power to control access through any part of the country. However, the target would not be an easy one: the hills in the area between the rivers and near the approaches to the bridges, plus the alignment of the bridges, dictated the attack tracks, making them predictable for the extensive AAA defences. In the immediate area, these included 90 heavy- and 45 small-calibre guns, making it one of the most heavily defended areas in North Korea. Defence suppression therefore became one of the most important aspects of the targeting each day. An intensive five-day campaign commenced on the night of January 9, when 18 B-29s escorted by F-94s bombed the bridges and marshalling yards between Yongmidong and Sinanju, while B-26s attacked AAA and searchlight batteries in the target area. Throughout the next day, there was an almost continuous attack by fighter-bombers, which flew 300 missions against the bridges and the defensive AAA positions. That evening, more raids by B-29s kept up the pressure on the railway centre at Namsi, the Sinhungdong bridge over the Chongchon River, some 70 miles upstream of Sinanju, and the rail marshalling yards to the south of Sinanju. Once again, the bombers were escorted, but they were intercepted over the target area by MiG-15s from the 351st and 535th IAPs. After being damaged by AAA fire, a B-29 from the 307th BG (44-61802), flown by Capt Arthur Heise, was finished off by MiGs.

No missions were flown against the chokepoint on January 11 because of poor weather, but the large-scale attacks continued throughout the following four days and nights. It was reckoned that eight fighter-bombers attacked the target array every minute. The missions flown on January 13 provide a good example of the pace of operations: during the previous night, 12 B-29s attacked the marshalling yards at Kwaksan and Chongju, supported by six B-26s carrying out harassing operations nearby, and five F-84s from the 49th and 58th FBGs attacked the searchlights.

In the morning, 114 fighter-bombers – comprising F-84s from the 49th, 58th and 474th FBGs, F-80s from the 8th FBG, and Panthers from MAG-33 – neutralized the AAA defences, while 122 F-86s provided fighter cover for 60 fighter-bombers as they dive-bombed the bridges. The attack opened at 0919hrs with nine F-84s from the 58th FBG bombing bridge B-66 over the Chongchon River, while just a minute later, eight F-84s from the 49th FBG struck bridge B-62 over the Taeryong River. In a second wave following just three minutes later, 12 F-80s from the 8th FBG attacked bridge B-67 over the Chongchon and 11 F-84s from the 58th FBG rolled in on bridge B-63 over the Taeryong. The bridges B-64 North and B-64 South (which crossed the Taeryong River via a small island rather than in a single span) were bombed by two waves of F-84s from the 474th FBG at 0928hrs and 0935hrs respectively. The ratio of 236 AAA-suppression and fighter-escort aircraft to just 60 strike aircraft is a good illustration of the importance attached to neutralizing the defences. The completion of the strike within a window of 16 minutes also demonstrated the ability of UNC to coordinate a complex attack plan successfully.

In the afternoon, the AAA suppression was carried out by 103 fighter-bombers, drawn from the same units as the morning wave, and the fighter cover was maintained once again by 122 F-86s. Six F-84s from the 58th FBG bombed the bridge B-74 over the Chongchon River at 1500hrs, but the rest of the effort that afternoon was directed against the bridges over the Taeryong River. At 1515hrs, seven F-84s from the 58th FBG and 12 more from the

Skyraiders of VA-115 from USS *Philippine Sea* set off for a mission over North Korea in early 1952. (Philip Jarrett)

474th FBG carried out simultaneous attacks on bridges B-63 and B-64 South respectively, followed two minutes later by six F-84s from the 49th FBG and 12 from the 58th FBG against bridges B-66 and B-67. In the next few minutes, bridge B-67 was hit by two more formations: three F-84s from the 58th FBG were followed over the target by 11 F-80s from the 8th FBG. The final attack was by 12 F-84s from the 474th FBG, which struck bridge B-64 North. During the day, UAA MiG-15s attempted to intervene, but they were driven off by the F-86s and two MiGs were shot down.

That night, 12 B-29s bombed the marshalling yards at Sinanju and Kunuri, while harassment attacks were conducted by eight B-26s from the 3rd BW(L) and four jets drawn from the 8th and 474th FBGs. A total of 1,166 sorties were flown in the five-day campaign, made up of 713 defence-suppression sorties and 453 strike sorties. The UNC defence-suppression tactics had worked well and losses were relatively light at only seven fighter-bombers. The western rail route was closed for six days, but reconnaissance sorties revealed that repair work was well underway by January 19 and the first bridges had been repaired by January 21; trucks were also spotted driving across the ice on the frozen rivers. Meanwhile, the North Korean AAA defences in the immediate area were strengthened, the number of guns increasing to 139 heavy- and 75 small-calibre weapons. The North Koreans also set about building a new rail track extending from Namsi to Kunuri and thence south to Chasan-ni, thus completely bypassing the Sinanju–Yongmidong Chokepoint and opening another route for the supply network to use. This 60-mile line was completed at an impressive rate of 1 mile per day.

Night-bombing missions by B-29s continued throughout late January. In the early hours of January 29, B-29 'Shady Lady/Double or Nuthin" (42-65357), flown by 1st Lt Gilbert L. Ashley, became the last Superfortress loss of the war when it was shot down by Soviet MiG-15 pilot Maj A. M. Karelin of the 351st IAP. The five crew members who bailed out of the aircraft were taken as prisoners, but the remaining nine were killed. Karelin was also credited with a B-29 kill on January 30, although in this case his quarry was able to make an emergency landing at Suwon.

Strikes on the North Korean hydroelectric power-generating system continued into 1953. On February 15, 22 F-84s from the 474th FBG bombed the generator house at the Suiho dam, and before dawn on May 3, Lt Cdr W. C. Griese led three Skyraiders from USS *Valley Forge* (CV-45) to bomb the Chosin Number 1 plant. Attacks against bridges continued too, and a strike by 18 B-29s against the bridges at Yongmidong on March 21 successfully dropped spans from two of the bridges. However, this campaign was curtailed after the follow-up attack the next night observed that one of the bridges had already been repaired.

Air Pressure – the irrigation dams

At the end of April, the armistice negotiations once again became deadlocked, and the UNC commanders looked for a means of applying strategic pressure on the DPRK leadership. It was decided that destruction of the dams which controlled the irrigation system in the Haeju peninsula would affect the rice production in the region and thereby demonstrate that the UNC could, if necessary, destroy the means of food production in North Korea. Since rice was the staple diet of the North Korean and Chinese troops, a rice shortage would also impact directly on the fighting capability of the CPVA and KPA. As a secondary effect, destruction of the dams would lead to flash floods which would wash away roadways and railway lines in the area. More than 20 small reservoirs fed the irrigation system that provided water to roughly 75 percent of the rice-growing region to the north of Pyongyang. Five of these dams were identified as being the most important: the Toksan dam on the Kyollyong reservoir, 5 miles north of Sunan; the Chasan dam on the Chamo reservoir, 6 miles southwest of Suncheon; the Kuwonga dam on the Imwon reservoir, about 7 miles north of Pyongyang; the Kusong

The following markings appear on the image:

B - Hammond
NC - Covi
R - 115 Over
D - O
EL - 115
I - 100.00
I - 12.50
BEI - 56.25

ANS Error D

SINANJU RR BY-PASS
1000 LB. G.P.

ACTUAL MPI

DESIRED MPI

The bridges over the Chongchon River at Sinuiju under attack again during an intensive five-day campaign that commenced on the night of January 9, 1953. (US National Archive)

dam, 5 miles west of Kusong; and the Toksang dam (not to be confused with the similarly named Toksan dam), 6 miles west of Taechon.

The first strike was against the Toksan dam. On the afternoon of May 13, 59 F-84s from the 58th FBG, flying in four waves, skip-bombed 1,000lb bombs onto the earth and stone structure from low level. Despite achieving good hits on the target, the pilots reported that the dam appeared to be undamaged. However, a follow-up mission the next morning found that the dam had collapsed during the night and the Potong River valley had flooded all the way to Pyongyang, washing away the main road and rail links between Pyongyang and the Yalu River. Sunan airfield had been inundated and 700 buildings destroyed. At a stroke, the attack had achieved what numerous interdiction sorties over the previous months had

Attack against Chunggangjin airfield, 27 July, 1953

An F-84G Thunderjet of the 474th Fighter Bomber Group releases two 1,000lb bombs as it dives towards the runway at the North Korean airfield at Chunggangjin, on the banks of the Yalu River. Just ahead, Col Joseph Davis, Jr, commander of 474th FBG and leading the mission, is pulling up from his attack. The number of military aircraft that would be allowed in Korea after the armistice was frozen at the number in the country at the time the armistice came into effect. So, as the conflict entered its final phase with the imminent signing of the armistice, UNC aircraft attempted to destroy all the airfields in North Korea, including those under construction, to ensure that no KPAF aircraft could be deployed there. Anti-airfield missions continued through 27 July, 1953, the last day of the conflict. That morning, Col Davis led 23 F-84s of 474th FBG to bomb the nearly completed airfield at Chunggangjin, on the south bank of the Yalu River, in the northernmost tip of North Korea. Col Davis' aircraft F-84G (serial number 51-10454), which was painted in the colours of all of the constituent squadrons of the 474th FBG, is now preserved at the National Museum of the USAF in Dayton, Ohio.

been trying to do. On May 15, 36 F-84s from the 58th FBG attacked the Chasan dam, but this raid did not affect the structure. The following day, three strikes were mounted by a total of 90 F-84s from the 58th FBG, dropping 1,000lb bombs. The first two attacks were unsuccessful, but the third wave breached the dam during the afternoon and once again, flood waters cut off communication routes and damaged the rice crop.

After a pause of a week, on the night of May 22, a force of seven B-29s dropped 56 2,000lb bombs on the Kuwonga dam. Despite accurate bombing, both this attack and another a week later were unsuccessful because the North Koreans had pre-emptively drained the reservoir. Another attempt was made by 14 B-29s on May 29, but once again the reservoir had been drained and the dam wall held.

The Suiho dam was also attacked twice during May when it became clear that the two generators were back online. On May 10, Col Warford led eight F-84s from the 474th FBG on a low-level attack on the generators house. Despite intense antiaircraft fire, the F-84 pilots bombed accurately without loss, but their efforts were in vain and the generators continued to run. On May 30 it was the turn of 12 F-86Fs from the 8th FBG, who approached the area at medium level, mimicking the fighter groups, before diving towards the dam and dropping their 1,000lb bombs. The tactic kept them safe from the antiaircraft gunners, who took them to be fighter aircraft and ignored them, but once again seemingly accurate bombing did not interrupt power generation at the dam.

The improvement in the weather had also enabled the campaign against the irrigation dams to continue, with strikes against the Kusong and Toksang dams on June 13. The Kusong dam was attacked by 54 F-84s late in the afternoon: the first wave of 26 F-84s

A breach in the Chasan dam on the Chamo reservoir, 6 miles southwest of Suncheon, which was attacked by three waves of 24 F-84s on May 15, 1953, during the campaign against the agricultural irrigation system. (US National Archive)

bombed near the center of the dam on the reservoir side, and they were followed ten minutes later by 28 F-84s who bombed the same section of the dam, but on the opposite side. The bombing was accurate, but the dam remained unbreeched. Forty minutes after the start of the attack on the Kusong dam, another 40 F-84s bombed the Toksang dam, again with little effect. Both dams were attacked again the next day. A force of 41 F-84s were tasked against the Kusong dam, but caused little damage, while the Toksang dam was bombed that night by ten B-29s, which dropped 120 1,000lb bombs, destroying numerous buildings but not damaging the dam wall. On June 16, eight F-84s and 16 USMC Corsairs did cut a deep trench across the Kusong dam, but it still held; however, when seven F-84s and 16 USMC Corsairs arrived for a final attack on June 18, they found that the reservoir had been drained by the North Koreans to minimize the effects of the bombing. Similarly, attacks on Toksang by eight F-84s, 16 Corsairs and 16 B-29s on June 18 were unsuccessful because any damage was quickly repaired, and once again the North Koreans had lowered the water level to reduce the vulnerability of the dam. On June 20, all further operations against the dams were called off in favour of strikes against railway facilities and supply centres.

Reconnaissance reports in April 1953 indicated that many of the airfields in North Korea were being repaired and would soon be usable once again. These included Sinmak, Haeju, Pyongyang East, Hamhung West, Namsi, Taechon, Pyongyang East, Sinuiju, Uiju, Hoeryong, Chunggangjin and Hyesanjin. Meanwhile, the armistice negotiations in Panmunjom had begun to make progress and prospects for a ceasefire improved dramatically. The armistice would include an article stating that each side would 'cease the introduction into Korea of reinforcing combat aircraft … provided however, that combat aircraft … which are destroyed, damaged, worn out, or used up during the period of the armistice may be replaced on the basis piece-for-piece of the same effectiveness and the same type'; in other words, the number of combat aircraft that the KPAF could deploy in North Korea in the future would be frozen at whatever level was current at the time that the ceasefire took effect. Thus, UNC commanders sensed an urgency in ensuring that a minimal military aviation capability remained in North Korea by the time any ceasefire was agreed. Efforts against the North Korean airfields commenced with a SHORAN-directed attack by B-29s on the night of June 10. The Panthers of Air Task Group 1 (ATG-1) bombed the airfields at Hyesanjin, Sondok and Kilchu on June 13. Over the next eight days, the remainder of targets on the list were attacked by both land- and carrier-based aircraft and, despite challenging weather, all the North Korean airfields except Hoeryong had been struck by June 23. However, the pressure needed to be maintained to keep the North Koreans from repairing the operating surfaces. Again, weather was a limiting factor, but attacks were resumed against Pyongyang Main, Namsi and Taechon on July 4 and 9. Naval aircraft bombed Sondok, Wonsan, Hoemun, Yonpo, Hyesanjin and Hamhung, and F-86s from the 8th and 18th FBGs attacked Sinuiju and Uiju each day between July 18 and 23, while F-84s from the 58th FBG attacked Pyong-ni. On the night of July 20, B-29s bombed Uiju, Sinuiju, Namsi, Taechon, Prong-ni, Pyongyang and Saamchan, and the following night 18 B-29s revisited Uiju, but then poor weather intervened once again until July 26. On that day, Banshees from USS *Lake Champlain* (CVA-39) attacked Hoeryong airfield.

Operations against the North Korean air bases continued into the day of the ceasefire itself. The armistice was signed at 1000hrs Korean time on the morning of July 27, declaring a ceasefire from 2200hrs. This gave the 5th AF and TF 77 just 12 hours to complete their campaign against the airfields. A strike by 24 F-84s from the 58th FBG attacked Kanggye, and simultaneously 23 F-84s from the 474th hit Chunggangjin (Chunggang) about 50 miles further north on the Yalu River. During the afternoon, a third strike by 24 F-84s of the 49th FBG, plus another 12 from the 58th and 474th FBGs, bombed Sunan. These were the last strategic counter-air missions flown during the conflict: at 2200hrs, combat operations on both sides were suspended.

ANALYSIS AND CONCLUSION

In late 1952, Col Joseph Davis, Jr, commanding the 474th FBG, named his F-84G 'Four Queens' after his wife, Ann, and his three daughters. The four queen playing cards on the left side of his aircraft represent a poker 'four-of-a-kind' hand. The colours on the nose, tail, and wingtips of the aircraft represent the three squadrons of the 474th FBG (428th FBS, red; 429th FBS, blue; 430th FBS, yellow). (NMUSAF)

In retrospect, the UNC strategic bombing campaign over North Korea can be divided into three separate phases: the 'classic' bombing of industrial centres in the autumn of 1950, the strategic interdiction campaign throughout 1951 until the summer of 1952, and the 'Air Pressure' campaign from mid-1952 until the ceasefire in 1953. The first two phases shared the same objective, the defeat of the KPA (and CPVA) through the application of air power, whereas the 'Air Pressure' phase was intended to hasten the signing of the armistice and ensure the best terms for South Korea.

In the late summer of 1950, the mounting of a strategic bombing campaign against the North Korean industrial base would have been the natural instinct of commanders who had fought in World War II. The successful campaigns against Germany and Japan were still fresh in the memory and a repeat performance would have also gone a long way to consolidating the position of the USAF as a service that was both separate and independent from the Army. However, North Korea was very different to the highly industrialized economies of Germany and Japan, for although its industrial base was sizable, it was already in an extremely poor state. Added to this, neighbouring Manchuria would always be an alternative source of manufactured articles (and munitions) if the North Korean factories could no longer produce them. Consequently, the destruction of industrial facilities would be unlikely to have the same strategic effect in North Korea as it had done in Germany and Japan in the previous decade.

This opening phase of the bombing campaign was hindered firstly by the general paucity of targets in North Korea and secondly by the inefficient targeting organization, which also diverted strategic bombers to inappropriate tactical tasks. The targeting problem was resolved relatively quickly and the strategic bombers of FEAF Bomber Command carried out their subsequent tasks with precision. In the early days of the war, the B-29s were virtually unopposed, and as Col James V. Edmundson, commander of the 22nd BG, pointed out, 'our bombing should have been good. We didn't have any opposition and the bombardiers had all the time in the world to make their bomb runs.' Having ordered FEAF Bomber Command

to attack industrial targets from the beginning of August, Gen Stratemeyer reported on September 15 that 'practically all of the military industrial targets strategically important to the enemy forces and to their war potential have been destroyed.'

The completion of the strategic task coincided with the defeat of the KPA on the battlefield. There is evidence that the destruction of the oil refinery and storage facilities at Wonsan had cut the supply of fuel to the KPA during the Naktong offensive, but the degree to which the bombing of industrial targets affected the war-fighting ability of the KPA remains unclear. Furthermore, the political need to limit the conflict to the Korean peninsula meant that the industrial facilities in China which also supported the North Korean war effort remained untouched. This phase of the bombing campaign can be regarded as a partial success: the North Korean industrial base was destroyed, but the vital facilities in China remained intact beyond the reach of the bomber crews.

The second phase of the strategic bombing campaign dovetailed into the various tactical interdiction campaigns (Interdiction Plan 4, followed by Operation *Strangle* and Operation *Saturate*). Now faced with increasingly effective enemy defences, FEAF bombers were eventually forced to operate at night in the skies over the northwestern corner of North Korea – 'MiG Alley.' Bombing in darkness meant that fewer bombers could be tasked against targets and that their bombing accuracy was also compromised. The complexity of the CPVA/KPA transportation and resupply network, comprising a vast web of roads, tracks and rail lines spread across the country – often in difficult terrain – also proved a major challenge. Furthermore, the KPA/CPVA proved themselves to be adept at concealing their supplies, vehicles and rail stock in tunnels or well-camouflaged hiding places. Bridges on the network proved to be particularly difficult targets, requiring accurate bombing with weapons large enough to cause damage to robust structures; the remarkable ability of the North Koreans to effect swift repairs or to construct bypass routes also meant that sustained bombing campaigns were needed even to close down routes for a few days.

Because of their ability to reach far into North Korea, and in particular the far northeast of the country, the naval aircraft of TF 77 were able to play an important part in the strategic

ABOVE LEFT
Col James V. Edmundson (seen here as a general), who commanded the 22nd BG during 1950, pointed out that the accuracy of early bombing operations was predictable because the bombers were unopposed. (NMUSAF)

ABOVE RIGHT
Admiral Ralph A. Ofstie, the commander of TF 77 during 1951, questioned the value of seemingly unfocused interdiction campaigns. (US National Archive)

General William P. Fisher, commanding FEAF Bomber Command from October 1952, expressed his frustration at the lack of strategic targets in North Korea by that stage of the war. (NMUSAF)

air offensive. But this widening of the offensive role took place at the same time that UNC fighter-bombers faced increasing threats, particularly from AAA fire. Admiral Ralph A. Ofstie, who commanded TF 77 during 1951, wrote: 'I am beginning to wonder about the value returned for the present sustained attacks in carrying on the interdiction program in Korea. It may well be that we are being hurt more as a consequence of the cost of this operation and the losses sustained … it may be advisable that we reduce the scale of our aircraft efforts of the forces present and restrict our air operations to those which can be assured of highly profitable targets.'

This view was echoed by General William P. Fisher, commanding FEAF Bomber Command from October 1952, who declared that 'the target problem over here is getting extremely difficult. We are generally operating now … with strike forces of about six airplanes. Even these [minor] targets are becoming scarcer and more dispersed all the time. In two and one-half years of this War everything of any size and importance has long since been destroyed, and we are now picking in the rubble. Of necessity, because of our complete air domination, the 'commies' have learned to disperse and dig in. Their rail situation is almost impossible, and I feel ineffective; their supply requirements are low in this stabilized situation. They move their supplies by night in trucks and hide them in caves, tunnels, revetments, etc by day. They have learned never to concentrate. The result of all this is that both the Fifth Air Force and ourselves are hard put to get at them effectively.'

While Operation *Saturate* had produced some creditable results in early 1952, in the end there were insufficient forces in theatre to sustain the level of operations needed to achieve complete success. Thus, the second phase of the strategic bombing campaign must be judged to have failed, for despite the best efforts of UNC aircrews, the massive breadth and complexity of the North Korean resupply network was simply too big to cover with the forces available.

By mid-1952, it had become apparent that air interdiction could not deliver the Chinese and North Korean capitulation for which the UNC commanders had hoped. The target planners would need to think more inventively to find a more effective way to employ UNC aircraft – to find the 'highly profitable targets' alluded to by Ofstie. The result was the concept of 'Air Pressure' in the third phase of the strategic bombing campaign, which proved to be a much more effective use of air power. Focused airstrikes by massed heavily protected formations against well-chosen targets were able to play a decisive part in the overall UNC strategy. These were also much more popular with aircrews and operational commanders, whose hard work and sacrifice on the interdiction programs had seemed to have little effect on the course of the war.

'The shift of emphasis from the rail interdiction program to important industrial and military targets has been, it is believed, an increased contribution to the overall United Nations effort. It has also been more in keeping with the inherent ability of a carrier task force to utilize surprise and keep the enemy off balance. The success of these attacks and the very considerable decrease in the losses of pilots and aircraft is proof of the wisdom of the present program of operations,' wrote Capt Paul D. Stroop of USS *Essex* in his report for September 1952.

Although all of the industrial targets in North Korea were reported as having been destroyed in late 1950, factories, warehouses, and bridges kept appearing on the bomber target lists throughout 1951 and 1952 – an indication perhaps of over-optimistic battle damage reporting by the UNC, but certainly of the resourcefulness of the North Koreans in repairing equipment and maintaining some degree of manufacturing output. It was this resourcefulness, more than anything, which limited the effectiveness of the strategic bombing and interdiction campaigns. Even when the 'Air Pressure' concept was brought to bear against bridges, for example against the Sinanju and Yongmidong bridges between January 10 and 15, 1953, FEAF Bomber Command reported that the 'ability of the enemy to repair bridges was just short of miraculous.' In that case, one arm of the rail line was out of service for just 11 days, by which time some bridges had already been repaired and a 60-mile rail track bypassing the whole area was being laid at a rate of 1 mile per day. Even after the devastating attacks on the North Korean hydroelectric power-generating system, regular follow-up attacks were needed because repair work soon re-established at least a partial service. Nevertheless, the third phase of the strategic bombing campaign should be seen as a success: at a time when the land forces were locked in a stalemate, air pressure was a major factor in persuading the North Koreans that further fighting was pointless.

In parallel with the three phases described above was a strategic counter-airfield campaign that was intended to stop the KPAF (and then the UAA) from using air bases within North Korea. From the first strikes against KPAF airfields in the summer of 1950 through to the attacks against airfields in the last days of the war, UNC bombers were remarkably efficient in denying all aircraft operating surfaces to the North Koreans and Chinese. Admittedly, these efforts were limited by the proscription of attacks against the MiG-15 bases in Manchuria, but even so it meant that UNC aircraft enjoyed air supremacy over the battlefield and much of the North Korean airspace outside 'MiG Alley.' This part of the campaign was also a success. Indeed, the course of the war may well have been different if the UAA had been able to operate closer to the battlefield and support their own ground forces or challenge UNC air operations over a wider area: in that case, UNC fighter-bombers would not have enjoyed free rein over the battlefield and the CPVA/KPA rear areas.

Two interesting points emerge from a comparison of the start of the air campaign over Korea in mid-1950 and its conclusion three years later. Firstly, early operations were hindered by inter-service prejudice within UNC leadership, whereas the successful operations from mid-1952 onwards reflected the ability and will of the

Capt Paul D. Stroop (seen here as a vice-admiral) commanded USS *Essex* during the conflict and was enthusiastic about the adoption of the 'Air Pressure' strategy. (US National Archive)

air, sea and ground commanders to work together. Secondly, the jet fighter-bomber proved itself to be a better tool for carrying out long-range strikes than the medium bomber; the latter carried a bigger load but was less accurate in delivery and more vulnerable to target defences than the former.

With the luxury of hindsight, there are five clear lessons to be learnt from the strategic bombing of North Korea:

1. A World War II-style bombing campaign against a partially industrialized economy is unlikely to prove decisive.
2. Interdiction against a wide and complex resupply system routed through difficult terrain requires massive force numbers if it is to be effective.
3. Neither strategic bombing nor interdiction can be fully effective if much of the enemy industrial base or source of resupply exist in a neighbouring country where it cannot be attacked.
4. It is essential to deny the enemy the opportunity to operate its aircraft freely within its own borders.
5. The ingenuity and ability of the enemy to repair damaged infrastructure must never be underestimated.

Unfortunately, it might be argued that all five of these lessons had to be relearnt during the Vietnam War in the subsequent decade.

FURTHER READING

For a major international conflict, there is surprisingly little written about the Korean War, and literature about the aerial conflict tends to be focused on a single perspective or aspect; however, *Korean Air War* (Michael Napier, Osprey, 2021) gives a good overall description of the air war at the operational level. For more detail about the USAF involvement, the official history, *The United States Air Force in Korea* (Robert F. Futrell, US Government Printing Office, 1981), provides much detail, both of operational minutiae and the command-and-control structures. The US Navy participation is covered in *The Naval Air War in Korea* (Richard P. Hellion, The Nautical & Aviation Publishing Co, 1986), while *Red Devils Over the Yalu* (Igor Seidov, Helion & Co, 2014) is an account of the Soviet experiences over Korea. Also written from the Soviet perspective, *The Last War of the Superfortresses* (Leonid Krylov & Yuriy Tepsurkaev, Helion & Co, 2016) describes the confrontation between the MiG-15 and the B-29. More detailed descriptions of the parts played by individual units can be found in the Osprey Air Combat series, in particular *B-29 Superfortress Units of the Korean War* (Robert F. Dorr, Osprey, 2012), *F9F Panther Units of the Korean War* (Warren E. Thompson, Osprey, 2014), *F-51 Mustang Units of the Korean War* (Warren E. Thompson, Osprey, 2015), *AD Skyraider Units of the Korean War* (Richard R. Burgess & Warren E. Thompson, Osprey, 2016), and *Soviet MiG-15 Aces of the Korean War* (Leonid Krylov & Yuriy Tepsurkaev, Osprey, 2008).

INDEX